CHEVRON and PIPE

Sea Scouts

HANDBOOK FOR CREW LEADERS

by Carl D. Lane

BOY SCOUTS OF AMERICA

FIRST EDITION
First Printing, November, 1941
Second Printing, March, 1942

5000342

Printing Statement:

Due to the very old age and scarcity of this book,
many of the pages may be hard to read due to the
blurring of the original text, possible missing pages,
missing text and other issues beyond our control.

Because this is such an important and rare work, we
believe it is best to reproduce this book regardless of
its original condition.

Thank you for your understanding.

DEDICATED
TO
THOSE UNSELFISH MEN
OF FAITH AND VISION
THE SEA SCOUT SKIPPERS
OF AMERICA
by
THEIR CREW LEADERS

TABLE OF CONTENTS

FOREWORD

THIS manual is a companion piece to THE SEA SCOUT MANUAL, written by the same author. It is a manual of leadership for the Crew Leaders of our Sea Scout Ships. It is to Sea Scouting what the HANDBOOK FOR PATROL LEADERS is to Scouting and is not to be considered a technical manual on Sea Scouting, for that is the purpose of THE SEA SCOUT MANUAL.

You who serve as Crew Leaders are responsible to your Skippers for the leadership of the members of your Crews. You have the responsibility to your fellow Crew members to give them the best of your efforts and your ability and through the use of this manual you have an opportunity to increase your capacity and effectiveness in the leadership of your Crew.

In our democratic form of government this principle of leadership is vital — that leadership comes from the group itself rather than from the outside. As a Crew Leader you are part and parcel of your Crew. You do not impose your leadership upon your fellow Crew members but, by the power of example, lead the way. You should bring to the members of your Crew through your loyalty and enthusiasm the spirit of the Ship — what we call Ship Spirit — so necessary in the success of every Sea Scout's experience.

The HANDBOOK FOR CREW LEADERS is aimed to help you, the Crew Leaders of our Sea Scout Ships, to grow in your positions of leadership and to carry ever before you the ideals of the Scout Oath and Scout Law.

James E. West

Chief Scout Executive and
Editor of BOYS' LIFE

1

INTRODUCTION

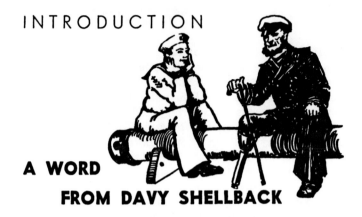

A WORD
FROM DAVY SHELLBACK

W ORD'S come for'ard. Lad! Yer to be leader o' yer Crew!

Put it thar, Messmate . . . Shake Old Davy's weather flipper, Lad! An' read with pride an' satisfaction the light in Old Davy's eyes. Davy's mighty proud o' ye, he is, Mate, an that's Gospel.

Crew Leader! Watch-master, Bo's'n! Yer persackly where ye allus dreamed o' bein', an' blast Old Davy fer a swab, he's been dreamin' likewise fer ye.

But yer not a leader yet, Laddy-mate.

Ye were given the berth only because yer Skipper *thinks* ye will make a leader. The trick, me bucko, is to stay there! An' that's why Old Davy fetched out his whalin' pi'ture for ye.

Ye'll notice Old Davy, Lad . . . han'some an' a dazzler he was then, sez I modest, eh, Mate? . . . braced in the foresheets, fair blisterin' with the eagerness to irun Mister Flukes. When ol' Bowhead felt that irun an' commenced shakin' hisself he made a almighty fuss, he did.

2

An' it was Old Davy's trick to stay there, too!

He never shook me from the foresheets, Lad — never onct did he move me!

Why, sez you? Well, here's why, sez I.

'Cause Old Davy had knowledge! He knew what he was doin', an' why an' what would happen if he didn't do it an' ALL ABOUT IT! I was leader o' me boat, fair fit to take me shipmates on adventure an' thrills and sport 'cause I had studied HOW TO LEAD. Snortin' hundred barrel whales was nothin'; gale an' berg-ice an' Cape Stiff Williwaws wasn't neither — Davy's crew blasted 'em all from their course an' sailed onward 'cause yer messmate knew how to lead.

He studied in books. He studied from his Skipper. He studied from doin'— an' then he dug deep inside hisself an' brought out that something that all leaders have in

addition to knowledge, an' he mixed 'em all up good an' there he was, Lad — Davy Shellback, Able Bodied, Watchmaster an' harpooner in the starb'd boat!

An' now me Sea Scout Mate is doin' the same.

It's fair courses an' no doldrums Old Davy wishes fer ye. Read the yeoman's pages as follows. There's good an' truth in 'em to mix with that something inside Davy was tellin' of.

What's inside, sez you? Davy don't know, Mate. Maybe it's pride in doin'. Maybe it's loyalty. Maybe it's the wish to be o' service. Maybe it's the drivin' spirit o' the old-time whalemen —

A DEAD WHALE OR A STOVE BOAT!

Davy hopes sincere it is. Ye'll irun all yer troubles an' ne'er have to worry a tinker about the boat if ye make that the spirit o' yer leadership!

fer joy and grate deeds
in yer new berth.
Davy Shellback A. B.

4

CHAPTER I

CREW LEADERSHIP

NO SKIPPER of the great clipper ships that carried The Flag of the United States on the seven seas ever made a successful voyage without faith in his ship.

No Scouter ever made a success of the Troop or the Ship which he led without faith in SCOUTING.

Faith in Your Crew

No Patrol Leader or Crew Leader ever made a success of the Patrol or Crew he led without faith in that group.

This is one of the cardinal rules of leadership: have faith in what you are doing, the group you hope to lead, and the objectives of that group.

You cannot get faith here nor from any book or individual.

But you, as a candidate for Crew leadership—and remember that Sea Scouting's deep-water friend, Davy Shellback, says that the trick is to stay there—must have faith; otherwise you would not have been selected from among your mates as a possible leader; otherwise you would not be reading this book as your guide.

And so we have assumed throughout these pages that you have faith in Scouting as a way of living; as a game; as a program of fun and adventure.

We have followed the belief, too, that the Scout Oath and the Scout Law, through your Troop and Ship membership, have become living beacons along your course and that you turn to them for guidance as the mariner turns to the great lighthouses as he steers his ship.

This is faith in what you are doing.

You must have faith in the group you are leading, that is the Crew. You must be fully "sold" on its usefulness to itself, the Ship and Sea Scouting. You must have no doubt that the Crew is a necessary and important part of this program of fun and adventure; that the democracy of Scouting extends from the National Council right down to the smallest division of the Sea Scout Ship, the Crew. You must realize that each one of your eight shipmates is anxious to have you show him the deepest and truest channel through Scouting. You must prove that you have a job, not an empty honor.

This is faith in the Crew.

Faith in Yourself

Lastly, but by no means least, you must have faith in yourself.

When your Skipper and his Mates called you aft to tell you that they believed you could become a Crew Leader, they did so because they had faith in you. They saw something in you that made you stand out as a leader. They saw something that they believed your Crew associates would look up to, admire, and take inspiration from. They did not do it without careful consideration.

You may be sure of that. You have some or all of the fundamental requirements of leadership—and your Ship's Officers have faith that, given experience and guidance and "hows," you, too, can lead.

Leadership Is Your Challenge

So leadership is a challenge to you; a chance to prove to yourself that you can lead your fellow Crew members. It is, perhaps, a glimpse into the future, a vision of things to come, for Crew leadership takes the same qualities and abilities that are necessary to lead in industry, science, the arts and the many walks of life.

Now, just how to take this faith, this will to lead, and make it into something useful to Scouting, to your Ship and to yourself, is the purpose of this handbook. It will give you what other leaders have found by experience to work best.

You will find many ideas and "hows," things to do and make, methods and suggestions, in the pages that follow. Except, as they apply to the Sea Scout Program in advancement, ceremony, uniforming, and requirements, they are not strict rules or regulations. Rather, let these things serve as challenges, as inspirations—as things for your Crew to do better than described herein. Only in the measure that you become original, that you make every faculty at your command work for your Crew, will your leadership become outstanding. And to become outstanding—to climb the Sea Scout Ladder to Mate and Skipper and Scoutmaster and Commodore —is what your aim should be. Then the fun and adventure of Scouting for you will be tripled; its objectives of building character and citizenship, for you, will become reality.

We have been discussing leadership in its very broadest aspects and from now on leadership will mean Crew leadership specifically and will include young men of the following Sea Scout ranks: Coxswain, Bo's'n's Mate, Bo's'n and their assistants, Yeomen, and members of the Emergency Service Corps, Officers of the Deck and Quartermasters.

THE SEA SCOUT MANUAL, sixth edition, will be frequently referred to and should be a companion volume of this as it is read and studied.

You "Take" and "Give" Directions

Just as the Scout has always made a good Sea Scout, so will the Crew member make a good Crew Leader. It is essential to be able to take directions before giving them.

Probably your ability to take directions was a large factor in your selection as a Crew Leader. But, remember you are still in a position where directions must be taken, where the importance of taking them from your seniors is still more important because it now effects not one but eight Sea Scouts.

Look at this picture of the tugs pulling a great log boom to the sawmill. The log boom is Scouting, its thousands of Patrols and Crews being taken on the course which will, just as the rough logs will emerge as planed and polished boards, eventually result in "finish" for them. See the "Crew Leader" tugs, pulling abreast of each other; see the "Mate tug" and the "Skipper tug," each out in front, pulling and leading the way. It would be a catastrophe if the "Skipper tug" broke down, wouldn't it? It would be bad enough if the "Mate tug" lost her rudder or cracked her shaft. But just think what would happen if the "Crew Leader tugs" should break down! The whole voyage would be threatened for the two tugs ahead couldn't move the log boom alone. Surely those "Crew Leader tugs," lashed as they are to both the other tugs and the boom, should they fail to pull, would form a heavy and perhaps fatal drag.

They must keep up their steam, keep pulling as hard as possible; take without question the whistle signals for turns and

CREW LEADERSHIP   9

maneuvers which the "Skipper tug" gives. Otherwise the log boom won't get to the sawmill; otherwise the teamwork of tugging, of leadership, will be ruined.

And it is this teamwork of leadership, this carrying out of directions which moves the successful Sea Scout Ship.

The "Manual" Shows the Way

Direction comes from the Sea Scout Program. On every page, except the inside cover, of THE SEA SCOUT MANUAL these directions appear. With these as motivation, your local Boy Scout Council (see Chapter 21, THE SEA SCOUT MANUAL), through your Skipper and his Mates will pass on the orders to you. And it becomes your duty to pass them on to your Crew in the form of fun, projects, things to do and make, service, adventure, cruising and all the things for which your Crew mates became Sea Scouts. It becomes your duty, to give your Crew the Sea Scout Program; to make it live and sing and shine for them—to give it not haphazardly, but with intelligence and in accord with directions that are given you or, as you, in your staff meetings with your fellow leaders, plan.

Leaders Pull Together

Thus these leadership tugs pull together, down straight channels, around bends, clear of shoals and snags, always following the foremost "Skipper tug." The log boom moves swiftly and safely.

But now let's look at the happenings

when the log boom nears its destination. Let us say that it is made up of three kinds of logs: pine, birch and oak. Each log must be processed differently and each takes individual attention. It becomes a task that one man alone cannot handle.

So signals are sent out by the "Skipper tug." The "Crew Leader tugs" each take part of the boom; the birch, the oak and the pine. They break the logs up into smaller booms which are easily handled by one tug. The tugs take them to the division of the sawmill equipped to process that particular kind of log.

This is the way the Sea Scout leadership team functions. All officers and leaders pull together for certain objectives. But at certain times during the meeting and during the off-Ship activities, the Ship breaks up into smaller groups, each with its own program and activity. These smaller groups are the Crews under leadership of you, the Crew Leader.

It is this group for which you are responsible, which looks to you as the next highest in rank. It is this particular part of the log boom which you must tug and pull and maneuver. If you do a good job of this your Crew and its members will

CREW LEADERSHIP   11

enjoy Sea Scouting. You will get the "finish" that the logs get at the sawmill.

You can now well see that failure to take orders or to follow directions, to pull with the other leaders to a common end, will result in disaster for yourself. But more than that, it will be a drag on the rest of the members of your Ship.

Sail Parallel Course With Ship

If you have promised yourself to pull with your fellow Crew Leaders, your Skipper, his Mates and Quartermasters, you have taken the first big step towards successful leadership. Your course through Sea Scouting will be a bright and happy one. In the boundless opportunities in the Sea Scout Program for you and your Crew to act and think and do, you will never lose sight of the rest of the Ship. You will sail a parallel course with her. As you do this you will find the other Crews of your Ship sailing along with you. And it is here that the real fun, the sport, of Crew leadership is found. For you will find that you will want to outsail these other Crews, you will want to sail on faster and truer—you will want your Crew to win! In devising ways to do this, in thinking up and accomplishing the projects, the service, the advancement, the exhibits and cruises and demonstrations —all the thousands of things that Sea Scouts do—you will find the joy of real leadership, the fellowship of being a co-leader, the satisfaction of hearing your

CHAPTER I

Skipper say to you, "Well done, Bo's'n!"

There is only one satisfaction greater—when someday your Ship is a Flagship, when you hear a Fleet officer say to your Skipper "Well done, Skipper!" To know then that you and the Crew which you lead contributed to that honor, pulled and helped and won for your Ship. That, Shipmate, is real joy! That is the reward of leadership!

Qualities of a Leader

The ideal leader in Sea Scouting is an "all-around man." He needs inherent qualities; he needs others which he can acquire; he may have some that he will have to lose.

Below is a self-analysis chart. Check off those qualifications that you honestly believe you have. Leave blank those which you do not have. Turn the corner of this page so that it can easily be found.

SELF ANALYSIS CHART
FOR CREW LEADERS

I HAVE	I AM	I LEAD BY
Uniformed	Patient	Example
Advanced	Fair	Preparation
Lived the scout oath and law	Unselfish	Advance study
Been Prepared	Honorable	Having pride
Cooperated	a gentleman	Having spirit
Given "Service"	a good Sport	Knowledge
	a "Buddy"	
	Loyal	

Now, DON'T EVER DO OR PLAN OR PROPOSE ANYTHING AS A CREW LEADER WITHOUT TURNING TO THIS PAGE AND LOOKING AT THOSE BLANK SPACES. As sure as whales spout, your undertaking will not be a one hundred per cent success in that measure that you have been unable to check off those blank spaces.

Just to be sure, for it is very difficult to evaluate yourself, ask your Skipper or one of your particular buddies in the Ship to check it.

Sea Scouting and Seamanship

No man can say which of these qualities is the most important. However, it is well to remember that seamanship is way down near the end of the list. It is a fine thing to know the art of seamanship as well or better than your Crewmates but it is not essential. Someday, have a talk about this with your Skipper. He will give you an idea of the difference between Sea Scouting and seamanship.

One of the most important qualities of a Crew Leader is that he be an example to the men he leads. Thus your own advancement should be kept up; it would hardly be fair to encourage your Crew to meet the Sea Scout Advancement Requirements and you lag. Your uniform should be correct and worn with approved insignia. You should be meticulous in your attention to Sea Scout Ceremony; in respect to officers and other Scouters; to re-

CHAPTER I

member always that you are a representative of the Boy Scouts of America and your conduct, good or bad, reflects upon thousands of other young men.

Quite naturally, too, you should be cheerful and honest and reverent; should have made the Scout way of living your own way. Courtesy, gentlemanliness and helpfulness are things far better taught by example than preaching.

Now, just one word of warning before we advance into the "meat" of Crew leadership.

Ranks Are Expression of Faith

The ranks of Coxs'n, Bo's'n's Mate, and Bo's'n are not achievment ranks. They are seldom given because of outstanding deeds, no matter how fine or how thrilling they may have been. The ranks are decidedly not rewards nor honors.

They are simply an expression of faith; a definite recognition that you "stand out," that you will get more out of Sea Scouting and Sea Scouting will get more out of you if you share the responsibilities of your Ship's leadership. In order to give you the authority to best do this job, a

CREW LEADERSHIP 15

rank senior to the men you are leading is bestowed upon you. It is an honor to be selected, of course, but it is an empty honor, becoming genuine and convincing to others *only* as you demonstrate that you are doing the job and justifying the trust that has been placed in you.

Show How—Don't Tell

You might fool your Mate or even your Skipper into thinking that you are a leader. You might do this for quite a time. But there are two people you can't fool for sixty seconds. Number one is the man you are leading and number two is yourself. Here are two tests for leadership.

A. If you do this, you are, or very soon will be a leader.

B. If you do this, you are not now and never will be a leader.

The whole secret of leadership is contained in these two pictures. Successful leaders SHOW HOW not TELL HOW.

And this handbook is going to SHOW you how to become what the chevrons on your arm and the bos'n's pipe in your blouse pocket say you are—A CREW LEADER!

CREW ORGANIZATION

THE Crew is a self-propelling unit of the Ship. It might be likened to one of the small launches carried by large vessels. It goes where the mother ship goes. At times, however, it may proceed upon its own course and under its own power, but still on the same business as the mother ship.

The strength of the Ship is dependent upon its Crews. The Crew is dependent upon the members who compose it.

Just as it is important for the Ship to have strong Crews, it is important for Crews to have strong members. Crews are sometimes weakened by being made up of members who do not properly belong in that particular Crew. Here are some of the tried and proved ways of forming a Crew.

Selection by Age

In a Crew of this kind all the members, except possibly the Crew Leader, are from the same age group. Thus, in the two-Crew Sea Scout Ship, Scouts of fifteen and sixteen are in one Crew and Scouts of seventeen and eighteen in the other.

It has one great advantage. The relative ages of its members do not change. The Crew has a reasonable chance of sailing the Sea Scout course intact. This is desirable from the standpoint of both the Ship and the Crew. The passage of time and the many adventures in fellowship of such a group of young men binds them together with strong ties and promotes a sense of loyalty that distinctly contributes to Ship strength. They have become "buddies" because their Crew mates, being the same age, have somewhat the same likes and dislikes, hobbies, interests and problems. Then, too, because they are generally in the same classes at school and Sunday School. In short, they belong to the same "gang" and this feeling of oneness is natural.

A disadvantage lies in the fact that when this unity is broken the entire Crew is liable to drop out of Sea Scouting at once. And, as young men must go on to college or into business and their time becomes less their own, there are bound to be those who cannot maintain an active membership in their Sea Scout Ship. The fellowship of such a group, close friends and buddies, in many cases since Troop days, is so close that those remaining feel its lack so greatly that they lose interest. Their first loyalty has been to the Crew and when the Crew is broken up, they find it difficult to transfer that loyalty to another Crew or even the Ship.

CHAPTER II

It might be said that such a Crew — selected according to age — is a three-year Crew. After that, leadership positions must be found for the remaining members if their interest in Sea Scouting is to be maintained.

Selection by Rank

Many Sea Scout Ships form their Crews according to rank. It makes for fast advancement and ease of instruction — each Crew member "talking the same language,' as it were.

It is perhaps the least desirable of all methods of Crew selection, for it discourages at the outset the democracy of Scouting and creates a group which is quite apt to become select or snobbish.

By placing a premium on advancement whereby each Sea Scout must advance in exact step with his mates much of the fun of the program is lost for the individual. In practice, such a Crew must surely be constantly changing, for Sea Scouts do not all advance in equal stride, and consequently there is never time to develop a true Crew spirit so essential to Ship spirit.

This means that the administration of the Crew by the Ship's officers is made more difficult by this constant changing.

And beyond all this, there is lost a golden opportunity for some splendid character-building — for the member of a one-rank Crew gives his loyalty to his own Crew and misses completely the chance to help his Shipmates who are of lesser rank.

CREW ORGANIZATION 19

Selection by Natural Groups

In this type of Crew, by far the most general, Sea Scouts of every age and rank are found. Because its make-up closely parallels Ship make-up, the Crew organization, spirit, methods and program help the Ship. The Crew runs itself by the same means that the Ship does.

The older Sea Scout helps the younger, the Able the green Apprentice; because of varied interests, ages, rank and personalities there is always something doing in such a Crew. The result of these things is Crew spirit.

In such Crews, the members are permitted to make their own Crew selection and quite naturally they pick the group with whom they are best acquainted, or the Crew which contains the particular buddy who first brought around the new

"One for all and all for one."

CHAPTER II

member to the Ship. They immediately become part of a group which is very likely the same natural group that they would and do associate with outside of Scouting. There is a minimum strain between the members of the Crew because they already know each other well and have made the adjustments necessary for them to act as a group.

Sometimes a Crew of this type can be subdivided, or two Crews formed from it, with members selected by neighborhood. Thus a natural play group from the north side of town would compose one Crew and a group from the south side of town another, but both groups would be made up by natural selection. If the rivalry that naturally exists between two such Crews is carefully guided, an intense Crew and Ship spirit will result.

Accept Every Man

As a Crew Leader you will be intensely interested in your Crew. You will want a word in its formation. This is your right. There is no doubt that you personally can have more fun, do more things with a group containing your pals and school classmates than with a Crew whose members are strangers to you.

Wise Sea Scout Leaders always give the Crew Leader a voice in selecting those of his Crew with whom he wishes to work. They cannot always grant your most minute wish and therefore it becomes your duty to accept into full fellowship every

Sea Scout in the Crew. To do otherwise would be to injure the entire Crew and certainly would make Sea Scouting unpleasant for the member you did not personally select. To take this member, often a new Sea Scout, as a challenge; as a "greenie" whom you are going to make into a fine Sea Scout, a close buddy and a good seaman, is the Scouting way of handling the situation.

Here is a good way to select a Crew. Blindfold the Crew Leader — have him select from the sound of the voice alone. He will at once recognize his buddies, of course, and select them. The remaining members will be selected then without regard to advancement, rank, uniformed, (or not), or age. If a lad has been selected, say a Sea Scout who has not uniformed yet or who has been slow in advancement — the Crew and the Crew Leader have at once created a job for themselves. How to accept this job, to encourage this Sea

CHAPTER II

Scout to uniform and advance and fight for his Crew, will be treated in later chapters.

Just as the Ship needs machinery to operate, so does the Crew need it. Every Crew should have, in addition to you as its leader; an Assistant Crew Leader, a Yeoman, and possibly a purser.

These can be appointed by yourself or elected by the Crew. In either case, a quarterdeck officer should sit in as advisor.

It might be a wise thing to make these temporary appointments until the Sea Scout has proved his willingness and ability to learn the job, just as you have been given the job of leadership. If the Yeoman understands that he will be judged on his record and his performance, say in three months, he will put in that extra effort, that desire to excel and "show the gang" which will make him a joy to all hands! He is a mighty asset to the Ship, for the Crew that keeps its own records of attendance, dues and advancement in top form is one that Skipper will remember when plum-duff is sent for'ard.

While the Crew Yeoman works closely with the Ship Yeoman, doing some of the detail work for him, the Assistant Crew Leader is under the particular supervision of the Crew Leader. Not only must he be ready to step into the Crew Leader's place during certain periods of the Ship meeting but he must also be ready to take over

CREW ORGANIZATION

completely in the Crew Leader's absence. Here are the qualifications and duties for these positions:

ASSISTANT CREW LEADER

The Assistant Crew Leader stands ready to take over for the Crew Leader when called. He knows every detail of his Crew's organization; he is skilled in Sea Scouting and is on his toes to advance both in the requirements and in his leadership ability. His cheery personality and good humor carry the Crew along with him as a happy Crew, a "going" Crew, and a loyal Crew.

YEOMAN AND PURSER

The Yeoman is the Crew's scribe and keeper of the records. Good Crew records mean good Ship records — so his job is big. He should be interested in the detail work that is so important in record keeping. He should be neat, especially in his penmanship. And he should show imagination in making his Crew's records more useful to his Crew Leader and the Ship's quarterdeck.

The Crew Leader should always include his assistant in his plans, explaining them fully. Indeed, not by telling but by doing, will the assistant learn quickest and the Crew Leader should often give him complete charge of the Crew or the Crew meeting or other activity. Assistant Crew Leaders are often selected junior in age or rank to the Crew Leader so that when the time comes for him to take over the Crew he will have had experience and his age will assure the Crew of his leadership for several years. If both the Assistant and the Crew Leader were of the same age, it is quite likely that at some time the Crew would find itself without both — and under the handicap of again training a new leader. (See THE SEA SCOUT MANUAL, Chapter 3.)

The Assistant Crew Leader should not be regarded entirely as extra help but as a successor to the Crew Leader.

It would be well here to open THE SEA SCOUT MANUAL and re-read Chapter 20, for we have much to cover in this handbook and cannot afford repeating what already has appeared on the subject of Leadership. Note particularly when, where and how Crews meet.

Every Sea Scout knows how the Crew functions in the Ship's meeting and its place in Sea Scout Ceremony. This, of course, is merely the "dress parade" of the Crew and in no wise reflects its true func-

CREW ORGANIZATION   25

tions. How to have a good Crew, one that dresses well and is truly representative of the Scout Movement is the subject of an entire chapter later on.

Crews meet during the Ship's meeting, and these meetings are of the utmost importance for in them is built the spirit, the camaraderie, the fellowship and the adventure of thinking, planning, doing and learning together. This, too, will have its own chapter later.

Have Fun Together

There is no limit to the other places where the Crew might meet and function as a Crew. Of course, Sea Scout Crews will want to cruise and camp and swim and hike together. And they will want to serve together — enter into contributing something as a group to their community, to Scouting, the school or the church.

It must be remembered that Crew activities of any kind require a certain amount of organization, of Crew machinery so that ways and means are always at hand ready for use.

Just as our launch left the mother Ship to go on a side trip of its own, the Crew must have a power plant, reserves, charts, safety devices, and log books so that it can meet any condition along the course. With the Crew now organized, its leaders selected, we can turn to some practical *hows* which will knit this group of Sea Scouts into a mighty Crew!

26

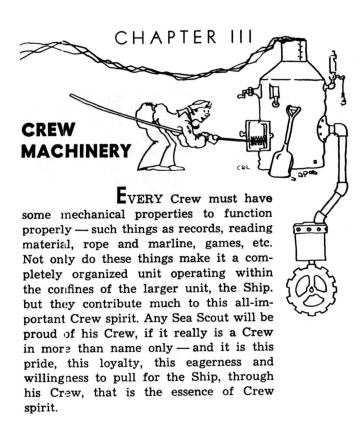

CHAPTER III

CREW MACHINERY

EVERY Crew must have some mechanical properties to function properly — such things as records, reading material, rope and marline, games, etc. Not only do these things make it a completely organized unit operating within the confines of the larger unit, the Ship, but they contribute much to this all-important Crew spirit. Any Sea Scout will be proud of his Crew, if it really is a Crew in more than name only — and it is this pride, this loyalty, this eagerness and willingness to pull for the Ship, through his Crew, that is the essence of Crew spirit.

Crew Records

It is not necessary for the Crew to have as elaborate records as the Ship. Indeed, a minimum of records, of paper work, is recommended so that Sea Scouting does not become bogged down in paper organization. The important thing to remember is that records must be accurate and up-to-date so that they will be of real use.

Naturally, the Crew Leader and the Yeoman of the Crew should be thoroughly familiar with Ship records, which are many, and the Yeoman should maintain the Crew records with the idea that he does not duplicate Ship records but supplements them, doing in the Crew some of the detail work which will permit Ship Officers to spend more time at Sea Scouting.

Crews, just like Patrols, collect their own dues and keep their own attendance records. This is done with dispatch, freeing the Crew to proceed with its Crew meeting and the Yeoman to confer with the Ship's Yeoman and Purser, or Treasurer.

The actual record may be kept in the *Troop Financial Record Book,* obtainable without cost from your Local Council Office. The book is passed from Crew to Crew, or carried about by the Ship's Yeoman, the records made and certified. There is a space to indicate the individual and total dues paid, and attendance is usually indicated by placing a check mark in the same box. The dues collected are immediately turned over to the Ship's Yeoman, who initials the total dues collected for the evening as his receipt.

Some Ships have developed standard forms for these records similar to the one below. They are fine — providing they do not interfere with Sea Scouting.

The important thing to remember about Crew records is not that the Crew maintains them but that the Crew and the Crew Leader use the facts which the records reveal.

Value of Records

Their value lies solely in their usefulness to the Ship, for when the Crew Leader and the Yeoman find from a study of the records that dues are not being paid promptly, nor attendance maintained — it is their job TO DO SOMETHING ABOUT IT.

It becomes the direct responsibility of the Crew Leader to see that his Crew is paying dues and is attending — the methods he uses and the results he attains depends upon how good a Crew Leader he is. The good Crew Leader, however, knows that he has, in a good Crew, one with real Crew spirit — an invaluable tool to make all the members play the game. He can appeal to the sense of fair play, for example, in the back-dues member and be sure that it will seldom fail. There may be justifiable excuses, of course — and here the Crew Leader, as he has much more time for each member of his Crew than the Skipper, can work out the situation on an equitable basis. Most decidedly no disciplinary measures should be taken, except after careful review of the case with the Ship Officers.

Generally speaking, if a Crew member fails to attend it is because YOU have failed to give him the kind of Sea Scouting that will keep him coming. If he fails to carry out his dues obligations, it is because YOU have not returned his dues to him in the form of fun, adventure, fellowship, and Scouting!

Crew Dues

Some Crews, always in addition to the self-determined Ship dues, collect Crew dues. These need not be great — perhaps ten cents a month — but they provide the wherewithal to enter upon Crew activities such as beach roasts, building a rowboat or sailing boat, Christmas baskets, etc. They are also kept in record form and some quarterdeck officer is made custodian of the funds, or a bank account is opened in the name of the Crew. Of course, it goes without saying, that the Crew should operate on a definite budget keeping expenditures within income; just as the Ship does.

Crew Leaders, and especially Crew Yeomen, are advised to read Chapter XIII on Ship's Papers, in the HANDBOOK FOR SKIPPERS, Chapter IV in the HANDBOOK FOR PATROL LEADERS, and "If You Are Yeoman," in Chapter 3 of THE SEA SCOUT MANUAL.

If the Crew is lucky enough to have its own Crew Corner or a more or less permanent meeting place, a wall chart on which to keep Crew advancement is a good idea. However, the Ship's quarters usually have such a chart displayed and it is a simple matter to use it — saving the time for its upkeep for Sea Scouting.

Come on, Record! Go find Trouble!

On the last page of Chapter 1 in THE SEA SCOUT MANUAL is an advancement chart for the use of each Sea Scout. This should be kept up. Each Sea Scout also has an individual advancement card and it is the duty of the Crew Leader to see that it agrees at all times with the advancement records of the Ship, making any necessary corrections during the staff meeting.

Cruise Records and Logs

Records of these types are highly specialized and are covered fully in Chapter 17 of THE SEA SCOUT MANUAL.

However, it is quite in order for the Crew to keep a log of every meeting, on the landship or elsewhere. These not only

CREW MACHINERY   31

form an interesting and instructive Crew exhibit, but are a source of inspiration to other Crews and other Ships. They might well include Crew photos, dance orders, programs, etc., and can become part of the Ship's log, which is submitted with the annual Ship Inspection and Rating Chart each January. The Harbor Log Form (Form C-687), obtainable from your Ship's officers at one cent each, is an excellent form on which to keep Crew records.

The Crew Leader's Ditty Box

By examining the Crew Leader's ditty box — usually a fair-sized sea chest — you can readily discover the interests, aims, hobbies, and goal of the Crew. In this chest are stowed the tools of the Crew — the material with which they work during and between Crew meetings.

Directions for making a ditty box are given in the supplement in the final pages of this handbook.

Here are some of the things it should contain:

SEA SCOUT MANUALS
Crew records
Knives for rope cutting and whittling
An assortment of rope and twine
Navigation instruments
Charts
Sea Scout Games
Ship chandlery, as needed
Signal flags
Canvas and sewing tools
Drawing materials

Soap and paper towels
Ring life buoy
Carpenter tools
First Aid kit
A whisk broom
Black shoe polish

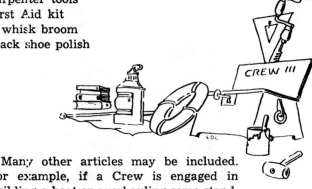

Many other articles may be included. For example, if a Crew is engaged in building a boat or overhauling some standing rigging, other tools and materials would be required. The sea chest, however, should have enough in it to meet the demands of any ordinary project upon which the Crew engages. A Crew carpenter might be detailed to be responsible for the contents, their stowage and upkeep.

Activity Builds Crew Spirit

The Crew Leader will see that many of the articles recommended for his ditty box are for use in meeting the Sea Scout Advancement Requirements. In the final pages of this handbook will be found many things to make and do with rope, tools and canvas Rope, for example, can provide almost endless projects in making belts, fenders, sennit work, ornamental panels, lanyards, etc. It is quite unnecessary to

CREW MACHINERY

continue the eternal knot-tying of so many Ship meetings. To use rope in a different manner than actually required for advancement purposes is to add sparkle and life to Sea Scouting — to keep your Crews attending and advancing, in other words, to build Crew spirit.

All the tools found in the Crew Leader's ditty box should be used with imagination and ingenuity; not merely to fulfill requirements. Thus, for example. when the Crew takes up the required project of building a schooner model there should be no limit set upon what a schooner model shall be. Let your Crew mates make it as large or as colorful or as detailed as they wish. The amount of time and effort — the conception and imagination — that goes into it is the fun and adventure of Sea Scouting. All young men are not mechanics, of course, but this in no way defeats the project. If the Sea Scout has had the experience of planning a schooner model, of doing the necessary research in THE SEA SCOUT MANUAL and other sources, of talking about it, thinking about it, asking questions about it; the fellowship of doing these things with his Crew — the real purposes of the requirement have been achieved.

It is the help that the skilled gives the unskilled, the inspiration that the Able gives the Apprentice, the competition of "doing" — even the ministrations of a buddy who applies the bandage on a pricked finger — that are the real reasons for the handicraft projects such as building a model boat, sextant, pelorus, and signal flags. Quite naturally every Crew Leader wants to have his Crew make fine outstanding things with his hands for at first glance these things would indicate a good Crew and a good Ship. But leaders who know how to judge outward evidences of the successful Ship are much happier to find twenty average pieces of handiwork than three museum pieces.

Your Crew Corner

It is a fortunate Crew, indeed, that can hold its Crew meetings in its own Crew corner or room. Not only do the Crew members retire to this space during the Ship meeting but they often gather here informally during the rest of the week.

In Chapter V we will discuss these Crew meetings more fully and suggest some simple Crew ceremonies and customs.

The Crew corner can well contain some or all of the following:
Crew flags
Desk for Yeoman
Work table, or bench
Seats for the Crew (and visitors)
The Crew sea chest
Wall decorations, sea pictures
U. S. Ensign on a staff
Ship's bell
Galley
Movie projector
Crew Log
Models made by the Crew
Library

CREW MACHINERY   35

The possession and maintenance of such a space will add materially to Crew spirit. Do you remember the thrill of having your own hut or cave back in Troop days? That was your castle — sacred to yourself and your buddies — and you worked long and hard to fix it up.

Following are some plans which might contain ideas for your own Crew quarters. Note how the one which is merely a railed-in section of the general meeting place can be made quite "cabin-y" and private.

The Crew itself maintains such a room, does its own cleaning and picking up, so that at inspection of quarters the Skipper will say, "Well done, Crew II !"

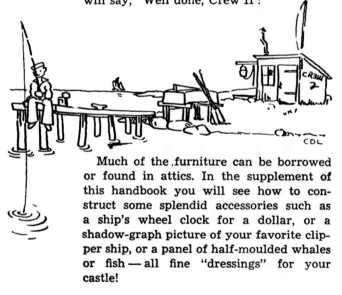

Much of the furniture can be borrowed or found in attics. In the supplement of this handbook you will see how to construct some splendid accessories such as a ship's wheel clock for a dollar, or a shadow-graph picture of your favorite clipper ship, or a panel of half-moulded whales or fish — all fine "dressings" for your castle!

CHAPTER III

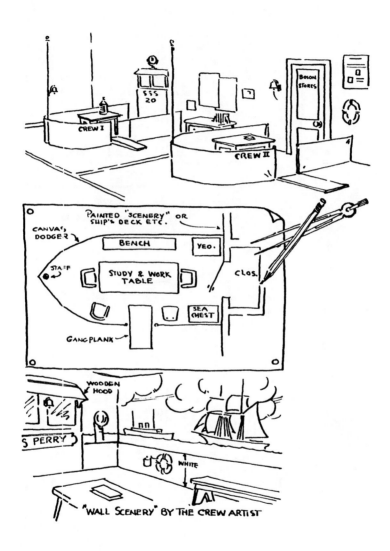

CREW MACHINERY   37

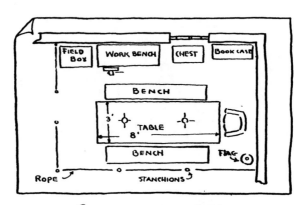

CREW MEETING SPACE
AND WORKSHOP

CHAPTER III

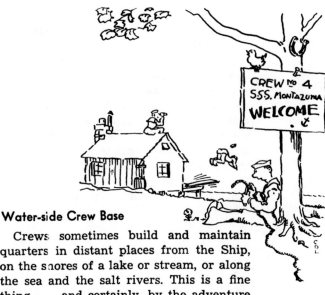

Water-side Crew Base

Crews sometimes build and maintain quarters in distant places from the Ship, on the shores of a lake or stream, or along the sea and the salt rivers. This is a fine thing . . . and certainly, by the adventure of ownership and partnership, cements the Crew into a close-knit group.

It is necessary to seek advice from Ship Leaders, and especially Scout Troop Leaders who are experienced campers, about such a Crew base. Your Council and the National Council have certain standards of sanitation, water-supply, accessibility, etc.. which must be maintained.

There are some ideas for a water-side Crew base on the preceding page.

The Crew Leader is referred to ADVENTURING FOR SENIOR SCOUTS for some excellent advice on camping by Patrols; the HANDBOOK FOR PATROL LEADERS; and Chapter 17 on Cruising in THE SEA SCOUT MANUAL.

CREW MACHINERY   **39**

Crew Leaders are cautioned against permitting the maintenance of either a Crew corner or an outside Crew base to reflect itself in "exclusiveness" or as being "high-hat." Within reason, the entire Ship membership should always be made welcome and no one Crew should ever withdraw, in spirit or action, from the Ship proper. One of the best safeguards is to invite one of the Ship's Officers, or Ship's Committee-men to act as your advisor and dean — just as your class in school has a faculty adviser.

The Crew is always a part of the Ship.

CHAPTER III

Every Crew likes to have its own library, a handy group of books and pamphlets which can be quickly referred to for instruction and enjoyment. Here are some really essential books which ought to be in every Ship's library. Those marked with an asterisk (*) could be very well included in the Crew library.

THE SEA SCOUT MANUAL*
THE SEA SCOUT PATROL
SEA SCOUT SUPPLY CATALOG*
ADVENTURING FOR SENIOR SCOUTS
SHIP RATING STANDARDS*
SIGNALING, Merit Badge Pamphlet*
COOKING, Merit Badge Pamphlet*
FIRST AID, Merit Badge Pamphlet*
HANDBOOK FOR BOYS*
SWIMMING, Merit Badge Pamphlet*
LIFE SAVING, Merit Badge Pamphlet*
SWIMMING, WATER SPORTS AND SAFETY
LUBBERS AFLOAT
BOAT BUILDING AND CANOE REPAIR
SEA SCOUTS AFLOAT
CREW LEADER'S HANDBOOK*
HANDBOOK FOR PATROL LEADERS
BOATOWNER'S SHEET ANCHOR

Of these, THE SEA SCOUT MANUAL is the most important to the Sea Scout in the ranks. The Crew Leader should make an effort to see to it that every member of the Crew has his own copy. Sea Scout advancement cannot be accomplished by studying at Ship meetings alone; home reading must be done and this necessitates having the Manual handy.

CREW MACHINERY 41

As the new Sea Scout joins the Crew, the Crew Leader should acquaint him with THE SEA SCOUT MANUAL, which will be of great importance to him for some years to come. He should read Part I in its entirety at once for there is much of inspiration there. Then he should prepare for the Apprentice Requirements.

As he climbs the advancement ladder, the Crew Leader should constantly stress, in assigned reading and instruction as well, that much more than the letter of the requirement is needed. Thus, to the Sea Scout studying anchors, while the requirement says merely to, "Describe three types of anchors — construct a working model of any type, "it should mean that he will read and study the chapter on Ground Tackle. In other words, the requirement is to teach seamanship, and certainly seamanship demands that anchors, as well as being described should be handled in practice, and all the gear and machinery required to anchor be thoroughly understood. It teaches by SHOWING—NOT TELLING.

The Merit Badge Pamphlets are necessary in Sea Scout Advancement and are to be studied to complete the requirements of Galley and First Aid, Swimming and Life Saving. The Ship or the Crew usually loans these pamphlets to the Sea Scout from their library. (See Chapter 4, THE SEA SCOUT MANUAL.) The handbook ADVENTURING FOR SENIOR SCOUTS has many fine suggestions for outdoor activities.

CHAPTER III

Too often the SHIP RATING STANDARDS is not secured from the Council office until December. The SHIP RATING STANDARDS is the best program help that any Ship or Crew can obtain. By showing in clear figures and records the exact standing of your Ship or Crew; by revealing both the weak and strong points, it indicates what kind of a program is needed to bring the group nearer the ideal. The primary purpose of the rating standard is not to use it in competition with other Ships but in competition with your own record of the preceding years! (See Chapter XIII. HANDBOOK FOR SKIPPERS) It shows where the Ship leaks, and where the leaks should be caulked. It gives the Crew Leader a handmade program. (See Chapter IV.)

The Crew Leader cannot better serve his Crew and his Ship than to adopt the SHIP RATING STANDARDS for his Crew. Just scratch out the word Ship wherever it appears — and write in Crew. Keep it up-to-date faithfully — starting in January — check it every month — discuss the results with your Skipper — and you cannot fail to have a good Crew. The Sea Scout Program is tried and true. IT NEVER FAILS. The failure is always that the Program has not been followed. The SHIP (*Crew*) RATING STANDARDS will show you where — and what to do about it. Of course it stands to reason that if you keep your Crew with a high rating, you are also helping the Ship in its rating.

CREW MACHINERY   43

Sea Stories You'll Enjoy

We cannot list here all of the fiction and sea stories that Sea Scouts enjoy. Encourage your Crew to read these brave, thrilling tales of the sea and of its heroes.

Sea literature is marked with a ruggedness, too often lacking in the plot laid on land. As a guide, here are Davy Shellback's ten favorite sea stories:

SAILING ALONE AROUND THE WORLD, by Joshua Slocum

MOBY DICK, by Herman Melville

LONG WHARF, by Howard Pease

TREASURE ISLAND, by Robert Louis Stevenson

BIRD OF DAWNING, by John Masefield

CAPTAIN BLOOD, by Rafael Sabatini

THE LIVELY LADY, by Kenneth L. Roberts

SEVEN SEAS ON A SHOESTRING, by Dwight Long

SAILING TO SEE. by Irving Johnson

SPOILERS OF THE SEA, by John Phillips Cranwell

The monthly magazines devoted to yachting contain many thrilling modern stories, as well as practical articles. The Crew might keep a back file of these, indexing them on the front cover with any interesting or instructive reading matter.

These magazines, obtainable at any news stand are YACHTING, RUDDER, MOTOR BOAT (Combined with POWER BOATING), NEW ENGLAND YACHTSMAN, PACIFIC MOTOR BOAT, THE BOATING INDUSTRY, BOAT AND EQUIPMENT NEWS, THE MARINE NEWS, THE YACHTING BULLETIN and THE SEA CHEST.

CHAPTER III

Boys' Life, Scouting's own magazine has many sea stories, both short and in serial form.

The National Sea Scout Log, which all Sea Scouters receive five times a year, has many *hows* for Crew use and contains inspirational articles by Sea Scouters from all over America. In each issue Davy Shellback, who is the oldest Sea Scout in the world, talks from his deep-water wisdom to Sea Scouts and Leaders alike.

Scouting, another monthly magazine which your Skipper and Mate receive, is intensely helpful to leaders. It is full to the 'wales with how-to-do's and suggestions, applicable to Troop and Ship. It has many articles, programs, projects and services of a Sea Scout nature. Crew Leaders should make it MUST reading, earmarking certain features to be read to the Crew itself.

How to Use the Tools

We have certainly discussed thoroughly some of the tools that the Crew needs to function with spirit and purpose. The Crew Leader will need a few suggestions as to how best to use them. Here are some pointed do's and don'ts:

The Crew Corner

Keep it clean and shipshape.

Keep announcements, log and records up to the minute.

Change wall decorations (pictures, charts, etc.) often.

Have seats for everybody — and extras for visitors.

CREW MACHINERY 45

Put tools in their places, sharpened and cleaned.

Strive always to keep it a department of the Ship — never a separate room, corner, or organization.

The Ditty Box

Have plenty of everything on hand (rope, twine, etc.).

Keep the shoe polish and whisk broom handy.

See that it contains, at all times, a Crew program for at least one month in advance.

Put one man in charge but do not lock it.

Crew Reading

Keep it up-to-date.

Trade with other Crews (especially sea fiction).

Put a librarian in charge.

If you (Crew Leaders) read to your Crews, follow these simple rules.

1. Always read to yourself what you plan to read to others.
2. Do not read too fast. Enunciate clearly.
3. Do not read for more than ten minutes (five is better).
4. Stop at a place with suspense — curiosity is a driving force. It may assure the Sea Scout attending next week or continue the reading for himself.
5. If you have read because you yourself do not understand the subject — DON'T, AFTER READING, PROCEED TO EXPLAIN IT!

CHAPTER III

6. Read, that is *tell* — only when you can't SHOW.

You Are A Key Man

You can readily understand now, that with two or four Crews, each equipped with the machinery of the Crew, each functioning efficiently and well — self-propelled, as it were, that the Sea Scout Program can be presented to the individual far better than if the Skipper were directly responsible for say, thirty-two men. Instead of one man trying to divide his time and interests by thirty-two, one man, the Crew Leader, divides his time and interest by only eight. Result: The Sea Scout Program goes just four times as far.

THE SKIPPER'S EXTRA FINGERS.

It is the heritage of every boy in America to have Scouting. The Ship with good Crew leadership or the Troop with good Patrol leadership frees that Skipper or the Scoutmaster and their helpers so that they can bring Scouting to more and more of those American boys who want it.

When a Crew Leader does his job, when he actually leads his Crew, he is saying in so many words, "Skipper, I will look out

CREW MACHINERY 47

for these eight Sea Scouts. Now, without hurting the Ship, you will have time to give Sea Scouting to every young man who wants to be a Sea Scout!"

Every Crew Leader makes it possible for every Skipper to lead EIGHT TIMES AS MANY Sea Scouts as he can without a Crew Leader.

Is your job worthwhile?

CHAPTER IV

THE STAFF MEETING

BILL JONES is going swimming. He looks at the time, estimates the weather, takes his bathing trunks and a bar of chocolate, pumps up the leaky tire on his bike and tells his mother that he will be back at 5:30.

Bill Jones in doing these things has planned.

He has decided where he is going, what he is going to do, how he is going to get there, when he will return and has even thought to consider that the weather might present an obstacle, that he will need food and that his leaky tire might present a hazard.

Bill Jones would probably make a good Crew Leader.

Bill might have started out for a ballgame, failed to state where he was going or when he would be back, drifted idly about the streets and ended up at the swimming hole anyway.

Then Bill probably wouldn't make a good Crew Leader.

Bill Jones hadn't planned.

And to plan is the secret of the success of every Sea Scout Crew, Ship, Squadron, Flotilla and Fleet that survives and makes Sea Scout history.

Planning Is Essential

To plan, in Sea Scouting, is to set goals and objectives, to prepare carefully to meet and conquer the obstacles which will threaten the completion of the plan, and to adopt best ways and means of carrying out the plan.

In Sea Scouting, one man can seldom make and carry out a complete Sea Scout plan. Planning is the work of several heads, of varied specialists, of all pulling for the same objective but each contributing that necessary part of himself which the plan demands. Such a communion of ideas and will, in Sea Scouting, is called a staff meeting.

The Ship Staff

The Crew Leader and his assistant are on the staff of their particular Ship. Also on the staff are the Skipper, the Mates, the Quartermasters, and invited specialists such as the Scout Commissioner, District Chairman or others.

The purpose of the staff meeting is for all the Sea Scout Leaders concerned to adopt and put into motion a plan or plans best calculated to forward the Sea Scout Program for that particular Ship.

Guiding the staff in their actions are these considerations:

CHAPTER IV

The National Program of Sea Scouting

The Regional Program of Sea Scouting including plans for special Regional events

The Council Program of Sea Scouting

The District Program of Sea Scouting as it relates to the Council Program.

The staff never meets to make new Sea Scout rules, requirements or interpretations but only to decide how, when and where the National Program of Sea Scouting, as it is given the Ship by the Council, shall be applied to that Ship.

And so, because the staff meeting concerns your Ship alone, because it thinks and plans for this fine group of young men who are your friends and buddies, it becomes one of the most enjoyable of all Sea Scout activities. In it, the Crew Leader can and does express his ideas, his ambitions for his Crew and his Ship and receives the group sanction to carry out his plans.

You will notice the staff, of which you are now a member, has not one plan but several plans, all keyed together and most carefully worked out. Suppose we look into these plans.

The Master Plan

This is a yearly plan, a full Sea Scout year mapped out, with dates and objectives set. To some extent it is flexible but by and large it is a "futurama" of what that Ship will do for a whole year.

It takes its foundation from the Council Sea Scout plan.

Thus, the Council has set dates for two Bridges of Honor, announced the opening date of the Scout Camp, set a date for a Field Day and made a cruising vessel available for a certain week in August.

Obviously, the District and the Ship can now adopt their own plans in order to get the most out of these events and would not plan anything that conflicts with these dates.

SEA SCOUT COMMITTEE

XYZ COUNCIL

COMMODORE'S OFFICE
Jan. 4, 1942

Sea Scout Program for '42

Febr. 2   Bridge of Honor & Ball.

Mar 29   Council Scout Rally.
          Inter-troop events.
June 3   Field Day (all troops & ships)

July 18   Sea Scout week at Scout Camp.

Aug 20   14-day cruise to Boston
Oct 1   Bridge of Honor & party
Dec 27   Commodore's Xmas party.

CHAPTER IV

This is a Council Program. Note that it is concerned with WHEN and WHERE. HOW is your Ship's Program!

Something To "Shoot" At

Now, the local Ships of the Council have something to "shoot" at in their own plans. First, there are two Bridges of Honor for which to prepare. This means an accent on the Sea Scout Advancement Requirements; also a drive for complete and correct uniforming, practice of the Sea Scout ceremonies for the public appearance on the landship. There is a Scout rally and a field day, both offering the Ship chances to participate in first aid, signaling, cooking and other Scout activities. The Ship Program will naturally train for the events in which the Ship will enter teams.

The Sea Scout week at camp suggests preparation for a review of Scouting achievements; also preparation to pass the requirements of Swimming, Safety and other Merit Badge subjects and to make some Scout advancement along with Sea Scouting. The week on the cruising vessel, would indicate a brush-up on navigation and seamanship, possibly some Crew project or a Ship event to make the money for this cruise.

One Ship's Yearly Plan

Now, here is the yearly plan of a local Ship of this Council. Note how, in addition to Council events, they have added activities of their own to round out and complete the program. See how they have carefully left room for a District Camporee which had been decided upon. Also, how they have added interest — how they have taught by SHOWING and not TELLING — by planning for minor events which will prove enjoyable to the Sea Scouts and at the same time prepare them for the main event.

S. S. S. DAVY JONES
PORT OF BAYSIDE

SHIP PROGRAM OUTLINE FOR 1942

MONTH	THEME
Jan.	Prepare for Bridge of Honor, Advancement, uniforming, ceremony. Recruiting drive for Opp.
Febr.	Make up teams for Council Rally. Signalling, Breeches Buoy. Prepare on M. B. subjects
Mar.	Review Troop ranks. Overhaul boats & camping gears.
April	Form ball team (District League) Accent School of Ship for Memorial Day parade. Launch all boats; practice pulling.
May	Fit out sail boats (Regatta May 30) Drill 8 oar crews for Field Day. Advancement drive.
June	District Field Day - all teams practice. (S. S. go in boats) Check on summer activities

Now the Ship has a complete program for the year. It must be further broken down, so that each month will be carefully planned and detailed. It is here that the Crew Leader is of tremendous help, not only in reporting his Crew's needs but its strong points as well.

As the yearly program is reduced, it becomes more detailed and personalized. The individual record of each Sea Scout is studied. Ways and means to help him enjoy the program and advance are decided upon. Definite assignments for each man on the staff are made. A large part of these will fall to the Crew Leader. It is the manner in which these orders are carried out, small drops that make up the full pail, that denotes the true Crew Leader and the real Sea Scout.

We find now that the staff meeting has before it a series of recommendations and suggestions. It will weed these out, selecting those which best tie in with the yearly program outline. Then it will decide upon ways and means to carry them out.

Personalize the Detailed Program

Here is a monthly program for four weeks. Note that the man in charge of each assignment is designated. It becomes his duty to see that all necessary arrangements are made and all material is on hand for the activity or project. The Ship, ever true to its Sea Scout oath of service, has included a worthy community project.

STAFF MEETING   55

Weekly Meeting Program

And now we come down to the weekly meeting program, which most concerns the Crew Leader and in which he takes such an important part. No longer does this weekly meeting appear a disconnected unplanned thing. It has real purpose, a goal and an objective. It is an intricate part of a whole but still interesting and fascinating in itself. It is the National Sea Scout Program, accented and intelligently applied to your own local Ship and her problems and standards.

It is alive; it has all the elements of romance and adventure and thrilling minutes. It now needs only LEADERSHIP to make it sing. It now needs only the word

SHIP MUSTER: Sept. 10 1942
S.S.S. DAVY JONES   XYZ COUNCIL

TIME	ACTIVITY	IN CHARGE	NOTES
7.25	Check shoes + dress	Crew Ldrs	
7.30	Opening Ceremony	Mate	(usual)
7.40	Announcements Dues.	2nd Mate Yeoman	(check last month)
7.50	Crew meetings		
	Crew 1 Drill	2nd Mate	
	Crew 2 Model Work	Crew L.	Have material on hand
	Crew 3 Visit Base	Mate	Lay up boat
	Crew 4 Splicing	Skipper	Use new rope
8.30	Talk by Adm. Dash	"	Prepare lantern + screen.
9.00	Sea Chanty - p. 242	Mate	Howlis accordian
9.10	Closing Ceremony Change the watch	2nd Mate " "	Check halyards
9.15	Staff meeting		
	Advancement report	mate	Notify Board of Review
	Discuss Oct. meeting activities Dance? Party?	} Staff	
9.45	Close		

STAFF MEETING   57

of the Skipper, passed smartly down to the Crew Leaders to make Sea Scouting a mighty force, a mighty adventure for those eager Sea Scouts standing straight and tall as the Skipper boards his Ship and greets these fellow-officers who are to help him.

The Crew Looks To You!

Any Sea Scout attending a meeting like this, if he analyzed what he and his Crew were doing, would find that it is the Sea Scout Program, cut down to suit his particular needs. It would prove itself a personal brand of Sea Scouting, shaped especially for him so that he will have the opportunity to contribute his strength, to brush up on his weaknesses, to play with and for the team and the league.

It could not be done without YOU, the Crew Leader!

We have so far spoken of an ideal, of the ultimate in Sea Scouting.

In practice there will be bumps and hard spots and discouragements.

They will not defeat the true Crew Leader, any more than the Skipper is defeated by the three or five or ten times as many responsibilities!

LEADERSHIP = LEAD-A-SHIP !

CHAPTER IV

These difficulties which are encountered can all be ironed out at the staff meeting. The wise Crew Leader will discuss them fully with his officers, being careful not to let his difficulties become personalized or in any way vindictive, and will always emerge with the considered adult opinion of experienced Sea Scouters.

It is entirely proper, and to be encouraged, that all Crew problems be freely talked over. A helping hand will always be found and a balm produced for the worst wound.

After a course has been decided upon, it is your duty to carry it out honestly and conscientiously, remembering always the Ship. No matter what; that must sail on and on!

Putting In Your Oar

The staff wants your ideas. It depends upon you for new twists, new projects, new ways to do old things. Give freely of your ideas! Be it a Ship or a Crew idea — talk it over; present it briefly and clearly, define the purpose. Scouting need never become hide-bound or stagnant. It is a vast laboratory in which to try out new and better ways of doing things — and from

many a Crew Leader have come ideas which are now part of the National Program!

STAFF MEETING

As a warning, never try a new idea until you have the full sanction of your superior officers. Sometimes, seemingly new ideas are really old and proven valueless or harmful.

Pulling Your Oar

After approval of your idea, even if it has been added to by others and becomes the composition of many other minds, keep your oar in and pull!

The other man has good ideas, too. Pull for his idea as you would expect him to pull for yours. Don't be out of stroke with the Ship. Work to achieve the smoothness and unity of a crack varsity rowing crew!

Tossing Your Oar

A boat crew tosses its oars at the end of its voyage. It is a mark of respect to the officers and the Ship; it is a silent cheer.

Never fail to toss your oars as a Crew Leader. Give the other fellow credit for a good idea or a grand job done. Take your own credit modestly and with dignity. Cheer loud and long, by voice and actions, for anything that helps the Ship.

That makes for Crew Spirit and Ship Spirit!

CHAPTER IV

With the Sea Scout Program defined down to actual *things to do*, you are now ready to put your part of the program into actual practice in the Crew.

We must, however, take time out to think about your Crew for a moment.

DISCIPLINE

Young men do not like the sound of the word discipline. Yet the Crew which isn't well disciplined through self-control isn't a happy Crew nor a successful Crew nor a Crew with real spirit.

This discipline is necessary wherever a group of people come together. Discipline is not a matter of bossing or giving orders. The word "self-control" is the real secret of discipline. When any group does things, not because you have made them do it, but because they want to do it, discipline will automatically follow.

Explaining the "why" of a situation, taking your Crew into your confidence, and making it feel that what it is doing is its own idea, not yours, goes a far way toward having a disciplined Crew. A sympathetic "why" in advance will save a disastrous attack of "whys" later.

The discipline which a Crew exhibits during formal periods, such as during ceremony, quickly carries over to informal periods.

It is something not to worry about. It will come naturally to the Crew which has spirit and can never be forced, particularly if it is confused with the outward evidences of discipline such as standing at attention, saluting, and giving an unnatural respect to rank.

The first step for the Crew Leader in building a disciplined Crew, is to understand thoroughly the personality and make-up of the individual members of his Crew. If the Crew is made up of eight Sea Scouts, there will be eight distinct personalities, each to be dealt with sympathetically and patiently. It is not simple, indeed, it is often very complex and baffling to study these individual young men. Yet the Crew Leader must make this effort just as his own superior officers have made the effort of studying him and the other junior leaders.

Here are some of the familiar types of boys.

The "Wise Guys"

Very few groups of any kind do not contain one or more of this type. He needs your special attention and sympathy. He is often at heart a "real guy," and through an unfortunate set of circumstances has had to adopt this peculiar twist as a defense. Probably the best way to handle

CHAPTER IV

the "wise guy" is to approach him privately; in public he really is a "wise guy" and has all the answers and cannot be defeated unless you yourself become a greater wise guy. Like many of his type he can often be helped by giving him a difficult job at which, without benefit of jeers or boos, he can learn for himself that actually he does not know all the answers.

"Easy" Types

In this group you will find the boys coming from pleasant, sympathetic homes where they have acquired a certain amount of tact, social ease and consideration for others. They are quick to conform, easy to lead and may or may not have ambition or initiative. Because Crew Leaders themselves so often measure into this type of "smooth running" personality, this type presents little difficulty.

In this class, too, is the passive boy. He never has an idea of his own. He never starts trouble and will follow docilely wherever led. You must study him closely, keep after him, encourage him to do things by himself whenever possible.

Clever and Keen

Then there is the clever fellow, the fellow who can quickly size up a situation and also size you up. He is often your keenest critic, he knows exactly where and why you failed, and, being clever, can probably do the job at least as good as you can.

If you don't mind your sheets and halyards you will find him quietly taking over the wheel in his own capable hands, running everything including you. This boy's cleverness should be utilized; he should have responsibility and a whole lot of it. Recognize his ability by taking him into your confidence, asking his advice, and appointing him as your special assistant. Be thankful that you have a young man like this and let him know it. He'll become one of the real props of the Crew.

Not-So-Easy Types

In this group the lazy fellow turns up. He's a pretty hard nut to crack. If he has been lazy in other activities of life, he will hardly mend his ways when he enters Sea Scouting. Sometimes, however, the lazy fellow has a great sense of loyalty. If you show him that his careless ways bring down the standards of the whole Crew and the Ship itself, he will often respond with a better attitude. If you succeed in pepping him up, never give him the chance to slip back into his old ways. Always keep him busy and above all keep him friendly.

The mischievous boy, too, falls into this group. This fellow is seldom malicious; he is simply lively; a fire-ball and a screwball and can't help getting himself and his Crew into constant trouble. The only cure for this fellow — and Bo's'n, he's a grand guy — is to give him something both interesting and difficult to keep him busy. Never let him have a dull moment which

CHAPTER IV

he can convert into mischief. Really, the problem of this fellow is too much spirit and vigor; it is not a difficult job to direct him in such a way that he will become an outstanding member of the Crew.

Difficult Types

Into this group fall the poor chaps who are really disagreeable. There is the grouchy fellow, and the bully, for example. These fellows are the ones who make sarcastic remarks, "get your goat," are domineering or brags. They need to be driven, to be shown how small and inconsiderate and unsportsmanlike they are.

This type, always a trial to the conscientious leader, often accounts for the discouraging moments through which every leader goes. Ask your Crew to help you in handling this type. Very often he needs the "works" to make him snap out of it.

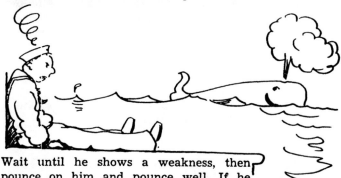

Wait until he shows a weakness, then pounce on him and pounce well. If he doesn't respond to a series of such treatments, he is a problem for your officers to handle.

Every Man Is Useful

Every type of fellow has some good in him; it can be brought out. So it is best, Bo's'n, to do the very best you can in helping all types adjust themselves to Crew life, remembering always that the usefulness of the Crew to itself, to the Ship and to Sea Scouting is never to be jeopardized.

Here are three suggestions for handling all types:

1. Keep each fellow busy at something that interests him.
2. Give each man some responsibilities.
3. Give each man your patience, sympathy, and understanding.

If, after you have tried all of these, you get no favorable reaction, and come to the unbiased conclusion that the erring member of your Crew is a serious drawback or even a danger, you may ask this fellow to withdraw. By all means first talk over the situation with your Crew and your Skipper. To be dropped from his Crew puts a bad stamp on a Sea Scout. It may be justice but nevertheless it hurts.

But, after all, it is better to cut a rotten plank out of a hull than to have the whole vessel destroyed.

The best possible advice to the Crew Leader is this: Treat every man in your Crew in the light of the Scout Law — you won't have many problems!

Bo's'n, that is your Crew!

Don't you honestly think that you're going to have a great time leading them?

CHAPTER IV

Don't you think that these plans which you make at staff meetings are going to be fun to put across, to see them register and bloom in these fellows of so many hues

Have you ever led a band?

You'd have the same problems there as you have now — blending those different instruments, some of them "unpretty" alone into a mighty sound of beauty and poetry and symphony called music.

Make these eight Sea Scouts into music, Bo's'n!

It's a job. It takes practice, but at the end of the concert there are bows and applause!

TWELVE QUESTIONS FOR A CREW LEADER

1. Do I know every Sea Scout in my Crew — his strong and his weak points; ambitions, home life, special needs?

2. Can I plan and conduct Crew Meetings worthwhile enough to insure steady attendance?

3. Can I report to the Mate at every muster, "All present and accounted for, Sir."?

4. Can I interest my Crew in continuous and thorough work for their advancement in Scouting and Sea Scouting?

5. Can I divide the actual leadership of the Crew so that every Sea Scout gets a chance to do his best part in helping my Crew?

6. Can I patiently handle the boneheads, the wise guys and the toughies so that they will come through with Crew spirit?

7. Can I keep the service idea strong in the minds of my Crew mates so that service is a habit?

8. Can I make the fellows proud of our Crew's appearance, dependability, and progress so that the Crew spirit will be strong and wholesome?

9. Can I plan a Crew activity well enough so that my Skipper can trust me to carry through without his supervision?

10. Can I wisely lead my Crew in its part of the Ship's enterprises and have enough ability to think through more things for my Crew to do?

11. Can I justify my Skipper's confidence in my loyal and thoughtful cooperation under his leadership for the development of the Ship?

12. Can I make my own life an unboastful example and encouragement to every man in my Crew?

CHAPTER IV

Service Outside the Crew

Crew Leaders, because of their special training and ability, have definite other niches in the Scout Organization into which their motto of Service often calls them.

Here are a few:

As Den Chiefs:

A fine service to the Cubs who will rise through the Troop to take your place some day. A Den Chief has as much fun as a Cub and he's doing a mighty important job. Work closely with Cub Leaders, forgetting the Scout and Sea Scout Programs entirely when acting as Den Chief, for Cubbing does not want to take the edge off Scouting for the young boy by giving him Troop Program before his Scout days.

Merit Badge Instructors:

The Crew Leader is peculiarly qualified to instruct Scouts seeking the Merit Badge in Seamanship. If a group, handle as you would a Crew, instructing from the Merit Badge pamphlet on Seamanship but giving them only the material contained in the pamphlet. To let these Scouts actually

STAFF MEETING

use Sea Scout equipment such as life rings, ice sticks, boats and other gear is a fine brotherly thing to do and will really engender a soft spot in the Scouts for the Ship into which they will someday graduate.

Guards, Watchmen:

At Scout Camporees, field days and camps, Sea Scouts are many times requested to act as regulatory officers. Do the job with sympathy and understanding and make your only badge of authority the courtesy and gentlemanliness which Sea Scouting has taught you. You will need no other weapon!

Aides to Sea Scout Officers and Distinguished Scouters:

Here is a job which almost invariably falls to the lot of the Crew Leader. And rightfully, for who can better represent his Ship or his Council than the man who actually leads the Sea Scouts?

In Chapter 3 of THE SEA SCOUT MANUAL will be found some pointers and the rules for the wearing of the aiguellettes of a Sea Scout aide.

THE CREW MEETING

The Crew meets in two places:

1. On the landship at the regular Ship meeting.

2. Other specially planned places.

Now that ought to be good news to any Crew Leader; to know that his time with these fine Sea Scouts is not limited to the brief hour or less each week when the Crew meets as a part of the Ship meeting.

One type of meeting is just as important as the other to Sea Scouting. Both are necessary for the wholesome, well-balanced Crew.

The Indoor or Ship-Crew Meeting

A well planned Ship's Program always allows for a period for each Crew to withdraw from the general group and to meet separately under the leadership of the Crew Leader following its own program.

The purpose of these shipboard meetings may be any of the following, but in all cases the meetings adhere closely to the spirit and objectives of the general

71

program adopted at the Staff Meeting.

Advancement   Social
Projects   Executive
Service

As Crew Leader you should come to these meetings prepared as follows:

With a program for the period

In uniform, on time, and with your SEA SCOUT MANUAL

With any material required

With boundless enthusiasm, good spirit and mighty plans!

The program for a Crew Meeting almost makes itself. The advancement chart will indicate to you exactly what the Crew as a group or as individuals require in the way of instruction. Your Ship Program will tell you of coming events for which your Crew will want to be prepared. The tastes, likes and hobbies of these Sea Scouts whom you know so well will tell you what to do for recreation, service and fellowship.

Perhaps there is no better place for Sea Scouts to prepare for advancement than at the Ship Crew meeting. The spirit of the sea, found on all good Ships, prevails; experts are at hand to instruct and demonstrate and the visible steps taken as each requirement is understood and achieved contributes to Ship and Crew spirit. A part of every Crew meeting should definitely be set aside for the general subject of Advancement. Chapter VII of this handbook is devoted to Advancement, giving the Crew Leader actual methods and projects to accomplish it.

Projects of a Sea Scout nature are logical activities for the Crew at their meetings. Thus, especially in the well-equipped Crew corner, model anchors, flags, sextant, boats, etc., might be made. The joy of actual craftsmanship in the fellowship of Sea Scouting is a great one. As the work progresses, there is bound to be considerable discussion which tends to make the Sea Scouts do their best. Competition keeps them active; planning new and better ways. Everyone wants to have the best model—and the result will be that they all will be good and every Sea Scout will have learned much about rigging, sails, or hull types.

The Crew Leader Directs

The Crew Leader need only direct such a work group. It teaches itself. Of course, the project which is undertaken should be assigned with due regard for the advancement chart. A few judicious questions — "Well, Bill, you tell me just why you think an old fashioned anchor will foul her warp" — "Okay, Hank, maybe a schooner is faster than a ketch off the wind. You tell me why" — and THE SEA SCOUT MANUAL will be opened, or the Skipper requested to settle the point — and there you have your Crew learning. They are interested, seeking facts with which to back up their arguments, perhaps arranging an ac-

CREW MEETING   **73**

tual sailing competition, or a visit to an old salt down on Dock Street, to prove their points. Here you have the real reason for the project method in Scouting; here you have the reason for the statement previously made that, "the important thing is to make it; not how it is made" and "to learn by doing."

Certainly, all projects made by the Crew should be kept on exhibit, correctly labelled and credit given to the maker. They are visible proof to the public and other Ships (and, Mates, to the inspecting officers each year!) of what your Crew is accomplishing.

More than a half million people saw the Scout exhibit at the New York World's Fair. Every article there was made by a Scout in his Patrol or Crew meeting!

Types of Service

Service, as the term is so gloriously understood by Sea Scouts, is service to others. Not often can such service be rendered at the indoor Crew meeting, but it can be planned there. It can be mapped out there. It can be organized there.

By all means, be ever alert to bring to your Crew the opportunity to be of service. Sometimes, the call will come from the quarterdeck, or from civic groups. Sometimes you will want to dig it up yourself. Talk it over with your Sea Scouts, report your findings to your Ship Officers and enter into it wholeheartedly. In the chapter on "Things for Crews to

CHAPTER V

Do," you will find many types of service in which your Crew can engage. However small, if it is freely given, efficiently undertaken and cheerfully engaged in, it is service.

There is a type of service to the Ship, though, which your Crew can engage in with satisfaction. Here are some:

Advanced Sea Scouts instruct Apprentices.

Make parts for the landship.

Cooperate with the Scout Troop, the Cub Pack.

Return (in the way of cleaning up, painting, lawn-mowing, etc.) some of the kindness shown you by the people who permit you to use their building for a meeting place.

Publish a Ship (or a Crew) paper.

Keep up, as your Crew's special duty, the Log book, wall decorations, records, exhibits, sea chests, brass polishing, etc.

(Fill out three more services which you think your Crew can do.)

....

....

....

Follow A Steady Course

The Crew as a social unit, as a gang of devoted buddies, takes care of itself. Even during work periods, the social aspects of the Crew are always in the foreground. And this is as it should be. It makes play of work; it makes fun of confining requirements.

Every Crew meeting should be a social gathering but it should be directed by the Crew Leader, not permitted to lapse into a mere hilarious shambles or a purposeless period of exaggerated good-fellowship. A common interest, a common project, a common cause or goal will prove far more binding in the long run than a mere communion of giggles and horse-play.

The Crew Leader should deliberately plan to introduce the light easy note into everything the Crew does. Nothing in Sea Scouting or in life is meant to be deadly and stifling. Laugh over what you are doing, take joy from it, do it with your heart as well as with your fingers and your brains.

One way to accomplish this is for the Crew Leader to plan much of his instruction through games. Friendly discussion groups, with arguments based upon research, is another. Demonstration by living models is another. Inviting authorities to speak and present subjects is still another.

The secret is to make live that which you wish to accomplish, to personalize it, to identify it with other human beings and with the man to whom you are presenting the subject. When instruction, projects, service, cruises, etc., are given this twist the spirit becomes more social.

A Crew which is socially well-adjusted, which has a good time doing things, is a Crew that has a large slice of this essential thing called Crew Spirit.

CHAPTER V

Of course, the social aspects of a Crew may take other forms of expression. Thus, there is no reason why one Crew should not entertain another, or give it a party, or challenge it to a match of some sort.

A Crew might well invite a Scout Patrol or a Cub Den or any group it wishes on a beach-roast, a party, a sail, a hike — or any activity the group might enjoy. The Crew members might invite their young lady friends to these affairs, with the permission of the quarterdeck, of course.

The Four S's

A word now, about the proper place of social activities in the Sea Scout Program.

Look at it this way, Bo's'n, there are four S's in Sea Scouting, three large and one small. The large ones are:

S—Seamanship
S—Scouting
S—Service

The small one is:

s—social

You now have the exact relationship of Sea Scout social life to the other sides of the program. There is no reason under the mizzen spanker why the first three S's can't be social in themselves. Certainly the fun and adventure of Scouting is a social adventure; certainly the thrill and education of seamanship is social adventure; certainly the experience of service is a social adventure. In fact Sea Scouting can survive without any social program.

On the other hand, it is a natural thing for young people to meet as a purely social group, and there is ample room within the program for such activity. The great danger, however, of the small social "s" is that it is permitted to grow into a large S and the moment it does the other S's shrink. So it is always wise to take the advice of The Sea Scout Manual and regard the "s" for social as dessert; an "s" only permitted to be used after the three more important S's are firmly established in the program of your Crew. The old shellbacks of full-rigger days could never have survived upon a ration of dessert alone, and this holds true in Sea Scouting as well. No Ship or Crew can survive on socials alone.

With this truth, ever flying from the monkey-staff of the Crew, it is urged that your Crew try a social. Few things will better cement it together into the close-knit unit your Ship needs you to be.

The "How" of Entertaining

Chapter XVIII of "Adventuring for Senior Scouts" deals in detail with social activities and presents complete outlines for some splendid affairs.

In the actual running of social affairs, the Crew social committee should keep the following few factors in mind to insure a satisfactory occasion.

1. Plan well in advance with your Senior officers.

2. Assign responsibility to Crew members

on a volunteer basis, i.e., let your Crew mates pick their own jobs.

3. Be certain that the place where the affair is to be held is suitable, enjoys a good name, makes no trespass on the religious sensibilities of any of the Sea Scouts or their guests, that it is decorated properly, heated and ventilated and otherwise made attractive.

4. Invite as chaperons some outstanding men and their wives.

5. By previous agreement maintain a level of appearance in the matter of uniforms or civilian clothing.

6. The hour of closing should be fixed in advance and should be one that will not cast discredit upon the Scout Movement in the minds of either parents or the community.

7. The Crew social committee should confer with some person of experience in the matter of planning satisfying and inexpensive refreshments.

8. Bear in mind, always, the cost, making it within the reach of all and giving honest and fair value to the Sea Scout dollars thus spent. Usually planning, time and enthusiasm will assure a successful social at a small cost of admission.

For the social within the Crew group, as a part of the Crew meeting, there are literally hundreds of Scout and Sea Scout games which make bright moments in every meeting. Many of them instruct as well.

In your SEA SCOUT MANUAL, Chapter 20, will be found a series of Sea Scout games that are real fun and can be turned to quickly.

In the HANDBOOK FOR PATROL LEADERS, Chapter X, will be found tried and true Scouting games that Scouts all over America play again and again.

Once again, remember, Bo's'n — the game is the DESSERT!!

And your Crew won't climb to the tops, or reef in a white-squall, or perhaps even tumble on deck with your call on a ration of dessert alone!

Sometimes Crews must meet in executive session. They must keep up their records of advancement, dues and attendance; consider and pass upon questions which effect them as a group.

This is fine but, oh, so very dangerous. Too many times, Crews do little else but these things under the fond belief that they are then acting as a Crew and accomplishing things.

A Word From Davy Shellback

"Oncet," (Davy says), "down off the Patagonia Grounds, me Bo's'n called me below an' he chin-wagged me fer a whole glass." "We need organization, Davy," he growls, "we need a record kep', an' maybe a common-fund an' no man's to do what he's sot on 'til he gams it over with his mates."

80   CHAPTER V

"We do, I agree," Davy sez, "but we got 'em. The skipper keeps a 'count book an' the log. To do it again would be a waste, sir."

"It'll bind the watch tergether, Davy," me Bo's'n sez.

"The watch is bound," Davy sez, an' takes the first o' the companion ladder, "the watch is bound tergether by work an' hardship and great deeds and lickin' mighty gales an' fendin' off berg-ice. Good-mornin' to ye, Will."

"Where ye goin', Davy?" the Bo's'n asks, cryin'-like.

"On deck," Davy snaps, "to get what I shipped for — the smell o' salt an' the music o' big-wind in the cringles an' the sight o' my ship shuckin' rainbows from her bows!

"An' I quit the black heart o' him who wanted to bog down Davy's adventure in bookwork an' yeoman chores!"

Bo's'n, there's truth in old Davy's words.

Here are some "hows" to use so that your Crew won't become "bogged" down in Yeoman records and executive duties; so that they'll have every precious moment left for what they shipped for, Sea Scouting!

Never keep any record that is not essential and vital.

Never make up records at Crew Meetings unless they can't be done at some other place.

CREW MEETING   81

Train your Crew Yeoman to work fast and silently in collecting dues and marking attendance.

Crew questions should be settled quickly and intelligently, never permitted to be reduced to off-the-point free-for-alls!

Allot not more than ten per cent of the Crew meeting time for this kind of work; strike a bell at the end of the time and stop it!

Crew Ceremony

It is fitting and highly desirable that each Crew evolve for itself a simple Crew ceremony, taking but a few moments of the meeting. It serves once more to impress the members with the fact that they are an organized group, acting as such, and that they have a duty and an allegiance to the Crew as well as the Ship. It is one of the many small things which go to make Crew spirit.

Here is a suggested Crew ceremony, for use when the Crew has retired to its Crew corner or Crew room or at meetings held away from the Ship. Another ceremony, more elaborate, will be found in the HANDBOOK FOR SKIPPERS, Chapter X.

Crew waits outside of the Crew meeting place.

Assistant Crew Leader "boards" the Crew boat, taking his place, standing, at the head of the table beyond which is a flagstaff.

CHAPTER V

Assistant Crew Leader: Crew (number), lay aboard!

Sea Scouts file on board, port side (if the space is physically arranged to do so), saluting in the usual boarding manner. Each takes his place, standing. The Yeoman has a place opposite the place reserved for the Crew Leader.

Assistant Crew Leader: Stand by to make colors!

Color Guards (two, previously selected) lay aft.

Assistant Crew Leader: Crew, to the colors! Salute!

Color guards raise ensign. Crew holding salute. Bugler or Bo's'n's pipe may sound off here, if desired.

Assistant Crew Leader: Two! *Then, when color guards have returned to their positions, Assistant Crew Leader says:* Stand by to receive (rank and name). *Crew comes smartly to attention, Crew Leader boards, saluting; his salute is returned by all the Crew and Crew Leader takes place.*

Crew Leader immediately details two Sea Scouts to side boy duty in preparation for the Skipper's weekly visit to the Crew.

Side Boys: Aye, aye, sir (saluting).

The Crew Leader may then go ahead with his planned Crew meeting, usually giving the command, "Crew, informal," which places the Crew on an informal basis until they are again called to attention.

CREW MEETING   83

The value of such a ceremony, and it may be elaborated or patterned more nearly after the Ship Ceremony if desired, is that more Sea Scouts have a part in it than they do in the Ship Ceremony and thus become proficient, so that, when given a duty in the Ship Ceremony, they will be thoroughly familiar with it. The Crew Closing Ceremony is just the reverse of the Opening Ceremony.

Receiving Ship's Officers

As Ship's Officers visit the Crew during the evening, the members of the Crew arise upon his appearance and salute, remaining standing until relieved by the visitor (which the considerate officer will do at once). All officers board on the starboard side. Visitors from the rank of Mate up are met with side boys at the gangway, with the Crew at strict attention as follows:

	No. of Side Boys
Skipper or Mate	2
Ship Committeemen	2
All local Scouters	4
All Regional Scouters	6
All National Scouters	8

Crews, at their meetings, might also adopt a station bill and hold practice drills in Fire, Man Overboard, Abandon Ship, etc. (see THE SEA SCOUT MANUAL, Chapter 18). This, too, contributes to smoothness in Ship drills of a similar nature.

CHAPTER V

During the Crew meeting, as has been said, the time should be planned and adhered to. The Crew Leader, relieved by the assistant (for practice and division of responsibilities) acts as director and, of course, is senior in rank and entitled to the respect of his Crew.

Some Meeting Programs

Here are a few Crew Meeting programs. Note how the accent is changed as the season changes.

WINTER

1. 8:00 (Strike Crew bell) Crew Muster and ceremony. (Indoors)
   8:05 Yeoman's minute (dues and records).
   8:10 Crew business session.
   8:15 Crew divided, according to advancement, and instructors assigned. Group teaching and demonstrating.
   8:30 All hands; work on model sextants (or other projects).
   * Collision Drill (no warning given).
   8:50 Crew Reading (a chapter of fiction).

CREW MEETING   **85**

8:55 Sea Promise, all hands.

8:56 Crew Closing Ceremony — lay aboard Ship.

JUNE

2. 8:00 (Strike Crew bell) Crew Muster and ceremony.

    8:05 Yeoman's minute (dues and records).

    8:10 Crew business session.

    8:15 Orders.

    8:15 Crew Closing Ceremony.

    8:20 All hands to base to varnish spars of Ship's launch.

    9:00 Return to landship.

AUGUST

3. 8:00 All hands lay to Waterside Park.

    8:10 Crew sing (have Buck bring his slide piano or banjo).

    8:30 Lay to dock for life boat drill. Apprentices to practice throwing life buoy ring.

CHAPTER V

8:40 All hands to refreshments (while
Yeoman collects dues!)
9:00 Rejoin Ship.

NOVEMBER

4. 8:00 Crew Muster and Ceremony.
   8:05 Pipe Skipper aboard; also Navy
Lieutenant who is to speak.
   8:07 Skipper's greeting to Crew and
introduction of visitor.
   8:10 Talk, with slides "Cruising the
South Seas on a 'Plane Carrier'."
   8:40 Question period.
   8:50 Crew business and Yeoman's minute.
   8:55 Crew Closing Ceremony.

CHRISTMAS

5. 8:00 Yeoman's minute.
   8:05 Crew Opening Ceremony with
Skipper piped on board.

CREW MEETING 87

8:10 Santa comes to Crew III — a PARTY!
Games. Chanties. Presents (or knocks) for all hands.

8:50 Abandon Ship Drill (without warning).

8:55 Crew Closing Ceremony; Skipper piped overside.

Davy Shellback Again

Bo's'n-lad, there's a trick in that last program ye'll do well to catch aholt on. That Abandon Ship drill, see? Back in my forecastle days, all good officers used it. Whenever they wanted us swabs to POSITIVELY give 'tention, they called a drill. An' we tumbled, lad, I'll say! They also used it when we give 'em a poser. "Bo's'n," Davy would say, seekin' learnin', "how can you prove the world is round?" An', blast me, Mates, the lubber would ring the fire alarm an' we never did get his answer. ('course, you wouldn't be tryin' that!)

Program Pointers

Here are some tips on Crew Program building.

Let every program contain always at least three of these eight features:

Business	Planning
Project (work)	Service
Recreation	Instruction
Ceremony	A reminder of SCOUTING.

Never repeat the same formula. Wait a few weeks.

Build to outshine the other Crew; the other Ship.

Build yourself into it as key man; plan

to earn the attention and respect of your Crew by your behavior as a gentleman, a Sea Scout and a friend. Do not depend upon your rank.

Crew Quarters

To the Crew lucky enough to have the space and opportunity to build for itself a separate and private Crew Room, goes the envy of every Sea Scout.

In doing this, you must work very closely with your Ship's Officers who must carefully consider cost, fire hazards, maintenance problems and Council meeting-place standards. As a Crew project, do the work yourself, gathering all the colorful nautical knick-knacks you can. And once more, don't become "snooty" about your Crew room. The stranger at your gangway should always be made welcome.

The Outdoor Crew Meeting

While much prominence has been given the indoor or Ship-Crew meeting the Skipper of our Honorary National Flagship, Dr. William C. Menninger has said that a Crew cannot hold too many meetings. And these additional or extra meetings are held away from the Ship, at a Crew member's home, at an officer's home or other meeting place, indoor or outdoors.

Its purpose is exactly the same as the other type of meeting, and the Crew Leader must have a program and also an objective.

It differs only in the fact that it is not a

CREW MEETING   89

part of the Ship meeting and that it may be held for a longer period.

It is at these extra meetings that the live Crew Leader can do his real job of leadership. Decisions and direction are entirely up to him. The time he can here devote to the individual, in instructing and inspiring him, is of real service to his Ship.

Indeed, so many of the Sea Scout Advancement Requirements can become real and vital only if the group studying them actually gets out and DOES them instead of merely reading about them.

Thus, such requirements as boat handling, signaling, cooking, navigation, Sea Scout drill and weather lore, to mention but a few, are far best prepared for by planning an off-Ship meeting and working in the field or on the water.

Time which suits the gang is the time for the meeting. It need not be at night, nor at regular stated intervals. Whenever there seems to be a reason for meeting — why, Bo's'n, call all hands!

You provide the program, mix some fun into it, request that uniforms be worn and the Sea Scout traditions be observed and you'll never worry for lack of attendance. These meetings need not always be formal, nor, for certain projects and programs, need the dress uniform be worn.

Too much is not suggested for these meetings. The Crew which has spirit, in the natural course of events, holds these extra meetings. The Crew Leader who has ambition, initiative and a definite goal, in

CHAPTER V

the natural course of events, calls these meetings. The Ship which has a program finds, in the natural course of events, that its Crews want to and do meet outside the Ship.

CREW MEETING CALENDAR

January: A Crew service.

A theater party (with the girl friends).

Start a Crew photo scrapbook.

Help a Scoutmaster instruct in Troop requirements.

Paint the landship.

February: Write a story of your Crew for the local paper.

Plan a Boy Scout Week party with the Cub Pack.

Check on the winter protection of the Ship's boat.

Make a Sea Scout model for local store window display.

Send a round-robin to your Regional Flagship.

CREW MEETING 91

March: Attend, as a group, a Council affair or meeting.

Check over the navigation gear of your boat.

Have a Crew picture taken for the Crew rooms.

Invite the fathers for a bean supper and Crew demonstration.

Attend your Church as a Crew.

April: Make up and adopt a Crew song or yell.

Get out the sails and air them.

Challenge another Crew to a Sea Scout contest.

Put on a Sea Scout demonstration for Senior Scouts.

Start a Crew movie.

May: Send Crew birthday greetings to Chief West, through Council office.

Brush up on water safety at a pool.

Take the Crew on a land hike, recall Scouting for them.

Paint the boat.

Work at the Sea Scout Base.

June: Hold a launching party.

Give a mixed party for members graduating from school.

CHAPTER V

Invite a Patrol for an afternoon sail and
chowder.

Start pulling practice.

Buoy a channel or erect a needed beacon.

July: Take an overnight cruise.

Attend the Council Camp as a group.

Clean up the waterfront.

Use a rainy evening to clean your uniform.

Visit a museum or historical point.

August: Send the full Crew to a Council
Regatta.

Check running rigging and anchor warp
on your boat.

Give the Cubs an afternoon party.

At an executive meeting, make Fall
plans.

Resolve that all hands shall swim in one
month.

September: Thoroughly clean the ship
meeting place.

Hold a beach roast for the Ship Committee and officers.

Unship the spars and sails, stowing them
for the winter.

Bring four new members to your Ship.

October: Haul the boat for the winter.

Make all new wall decorations for the
Crew room.

Put on a short sketch or play for the
Ship or Troop.

Do a community service.

Attend a football game in uniform.

November: Bring all Crew records up to
the minute.

Hold a surprise party for some mate's

birthday or have a Thanksgiving party with fancy decorations and special eats.

Study the stars some bright night.

Spend a full day working at the Council Camp.

Remove and paint all the boat gear.

December: Plan a Christmas Good Turn.

Check all fire exits at the Ship meeting place.

Make a sign for your Crew room with your Crew number.

Play Santa for a Cub Pack.

Attend Christmas eve church services as a Crew.

CHAPTER VI

BoTE

HOW TO HAVE
A GOOD CREW

"A GOOD Crew," Davy Shellback once wrote to his Sea Scout mateys, "always *looks* like a good Crew. A poor Crew, always *looks* like a poor Crew."

Bo's'n, that's the truth!

The good Crew is the Crew with Crew spirit; which is a Crew in much more than name only. Preceding chapters have been much concerned with this Crew spirit, this inner "something" which is so necessary and desirable in any group, be it Sea Scouting, Scouting or Cubbing.

If it is really there — and it is hoped that by now the Crew Leader, by his program and leadership has been shown how to put some of it there — it will shine through and make itself evident.

The real Sea Scout Crew can be recognized, not only by what it does and says, but by its looks, its appearance. It is recognizable, even to those not close to Scouting, by the way in which it:

Uniforms.

Carries out Sea Scout Ceremony.

Carries out Sea Scout tradition.

Represents the Boy Scout Movement in the matters of courtesy, gentlemanliness and Scout living.

The Sea Scout Uniform

A blue sailor's uniform does not make the wearer a Sea Scout!

It only indicates to anyone seeing or meeting the wearer that beneath the honorable blue beats a heart that is striving to make itself worthy of that uniform!

To the Crew which has spirit, which has made SCOUTING A WAY OF LIVING, which has seriously dedicated itself to the six "I wills" of the suggested Senior Scout Citizen's Dedication, the ownership and correct wearing of the uniform, will be one of its first desires. It will want to SHOW, that it is a good Crew.

It becomes the responsibility of the Crew Leader to see that every member of his Crew owns a uniform as quickly as possible, then, that he wears it correctly, with the correct insignia, shoes, socks, hat and neckerchief.

One of the very best ways in which to accomplish this is for the Crew Leader himself to own the Sea Scout Uniform and wear it correctly.

The next page gives all the information about your uniform and insignia.

Official Outfit

The correct Sea Scout Uniform may be either of blue wool or white duck. Some

CHAPTER VI

Ships wear blue at all times, others shift to white duck in the summer months, still others, such as Ships in Florida, the Gulf states, or California, wear white duck the year round. The complete uniform in either material consists of:

The Sea Scout Bob Evans' hat, on the foreband of which is embroidered the Sea Scout Emblem.

The Sea Scout jumper, on the right breast of which is an embroidered strip lettered "Sea Scouts, BSA."

A Sea Scout Emblem is in each corner of the collar. Both sleeves and the collar have two white stripes.

The Sea Scout Neckerchief, blue with either wool or duck, bears a stenciled Sea Scout Emblem in white.

Bell-bottom Sea Scout trousers.

Black socks of any material.

Black shoes, high or low, rubber or leather soles.

The National Supply Service of the Boy Scouts of America is the only possible source from which to obtain the Official Uniform. Listed in its catalogue also are work uniforms, jumpers and sweaters which are entirely correct for Sea Scouts to wears. Leggings are not a part of the Official Uniform, though they may be worn at the option of the Ship.

Upon this Uniform and forming a part of it are worn the Official Insignia and Badges noted in the following pages. There is one way to wear insignia — *correctly*.

THE SEA SCOUT MANUAL gives all the

A GOOD CREW   97

HOW TO WEAR YC

The diagram on this page shows the part of the left sleeve on which is worn the Community Strip, Ship Numeral, and Cruise Badge. These diagrams are full sized so that you may hold them up to your

LEFT BREAST POCKET

Service Stars worn with ⅜ inch showing between felt and top of pocket, stars ¾ inch apart center to center.

The Quartermaster Badge is centered above the pocket. If worn with Eagle Scout Badge, the Eagle Badge is worn to the right.

Long Cruise Badge shown with Additional Cruise Bar

Special Long Cruise Badge

LEFT SLEEVE

SCOUT BADGES

shoulder to get the actual measurements for placing your badges.

This page shows the right sleeve on which is worn the Ship Medallion and the Badge of Office or Rank.

Rank is shown by the number of bars worn under the Sea Scout Badge.

Apprentice

Ordinary

Able

The Badges of Office are worn in the same position as the Badges of Rank.

A Crew Leader substitutes chevrons for the bars of his Badge of Rank.

Coxswain

Boatswain's Mate

Boatswain

Yeoman

Bugler

Yeoman and Bugler badges are worn on right sleeve 4 inches above lower edge of cuff.

RIGHT SLEEVE

details for the care of the Sea Scout Uniform. It is the Crew Leader's duty to see that each member of his Crew is frequently instructed from these pages. The good Crew Leader often makes a drill of folding the uniform, instructing as the drill goes forward.

Members of the Crew should make it a habit to fold the uniform properly upon reaching home after the Crew or Ship muster. It is only by doing this that the uniform, when again needed, will shake out smooth and unwrinkled and with proper collar and trouser creases.

In other parts of this book will be found some helpful articles which the Crew might well include in its sea chest or ditty box to assure the uniform being clean and neat.

Black Shoes a "Must"

A word about shoes. Black shoes either high or low, neatly laced and properly polished are the only correct shoes to wear with the Sea Scout Uniform. Too often for perfectly just reasons, Sea Scouts are inclined to slip up in this matter of black shoes, claiming that they don't ordinarily wear black shoes or that they are still growing and would not get full use out of black shoes purchased exclusively for Sea Scout use. It is not a difficult nor an expensive matter for tan or brown shoes to be dyed black and polished, and the Crew Leader might well suggest such

CHAPTER VI

a course to the fellow who does not own nor wear black shoes.

The Sea Scout hat is a durable and weatherproof piece of clothing. When it becomes dirty or ragged it is usually because it has been used as a football, basketball or a dusting cloth. Such use is usually under the eyes of the Crew Leader. He is in a position to stop it instantly.

Many Ships have a uniform "slop-chest." This is a system whereby a Sea Scout, as he grows, may turn his uniform in for use of the younger fellows and in return get one which better fits him. This is a splendid and workable idea and assures a neat and trim appearing Crew at all times. Usually such an exchange is subject to a service fee of a dollar or so to pay for a thorough dry cleaning and any other expense involved. Sea Scouts who are leaving the Ship to go on to college or into business or who, as leaders, will need officer uniforms are encouraged to present their uniforms to the Ship's "slop-chest."

Sea Scout Insignia and Badges

Insignia is supplied for both white or blue uniforms and can be obtained only through the Ship's officers or the Local Council with a written note from the Sea Scout Leader. Scout Outfitters do not sell badges or insignia.

In addition to this insignia and as a reminder of their unique position in a fine and mighty youth organization, Sea Scouts often wear a civilian Sea Scout button on their coat lapel. This is a metal pin obtained from the National Supply Service at nominal cost.

The Sea Scout Uniform IS Worn

1. In all formal Scouting activities, specifically Patrol, Troop, or Ship Meetings, hikes, cruises, camps, regattas, rallies, demonstrations, etc. Also, at special church services for Scouts.

2. When preparing for advancement in Sea Scout Rank before a formal Bridge of Honor, or in the presentation of awards.

3. During Boy Scout Week in February.

4. When on duty for special Scouting service or civic service activity.

5. On such other occasions as may be specifically recommended or prescribed by either the Local or the National Council.

6. At formal Sea Scout occasions.

When the Uniform Should Not Be Worn

1. When soliciting funds or when engaged in any selling campaign or in any commercial operation.

2. When engaged in any distinctive political endeavor.

3. When appearing upon the stage professionally without specific authority from the Executive Board of the National Council.

4. When taking part in parades except for the purpose of rendering service as a Scout or Scouter, or as an official representative of the Boy Scouts of America.

5. When one has ceased to be a Scout

or a Scouter, through failure to re-register, or has left the Scout Movement for any other reason.

The uniform of the Crew Leader, whether he be Coxs'n, Bo's'n's Mate or Bo's'n, is exactly like the Sea Scout Uniform except as follows:

Sleeve Insignia

The Badge of Rank also becomes a Badge of Office by substituting chevrons for the usual bars. It is worn exactly where the Sea Scout Badge of Rank is worn: on the right jumper sleeve, the top five inches below the shoulder seam and centered on the arm.

Crew Leader of Apprentice rank — Coxs'n — S. S. Badge over one chevron.

Crew Leader of Ordinary rank—Bo's'n's Mate — S. S. Badge over two chevrons.

Crew Leader of Able rank — Bo's'n — S. S. Badge over three chevrons. (See pages 98-99.)

Crew Leader of Quartermaster rank — Quartermaster — Officer's Uniform.

Distinguishing Insignia

In addition to this distinguishing insignia, the Crew Leader of all ranks (except Quartermaster) wears a Bo's'n pipe and lanyard.

It is kept carefully polished, the lanyard always clean and except when in use, tucked into the jumper pocket. It is worn only as shown on the following page.

The Crew Leader should familiarize himself with the distinguishing insignia of Sea

A GOOD CREW 103

Scout Officers so that he and his Crew stand ready to pay the proper respect to their rank. (Chapter 2 of THE SEA SCOUT MANUAL clearly presents this.)

PIPE LANYARD LOOP PASSED OVER NECKERCHIEF. SLIDE BETWEEN KNOT & COLLAR "V". FALL PASSED BEHIND KNOT.

Inspecting the Crew

At frequent intervals, either at Crew meetings or before the muster of the Ship meeting, the Crew Leader will be called upon to inspect his Crew.

There is an art to this, understood by all good officers. Most emphatically, a Sea Scout cannot be bawled out for some carelessness in his personal appearance. This art of inspecting is based on two very simple truths:

1. The person inspecting must himself be impeccable: in no way guilty of the breaches for which he is inspecting.

2. Any infractions are to be noted but not mentioned, and privately, in a manner best suited to the erring individual, his faults pointed out.

You will have noticed that your Ship's Officers, as they make their periodical inspections of the ranks NEVER speak to a man in the ranks unless they have something complimentary or favorable to say. This is based upon the principle that all individuals like, and are entitled to praise before their fellows but that no matter how wrong, they resent criticism.

This is human nature.

Yet this same individual, spoken to in private, on a man-to-man basis will "take it" and usually take immediate steps to correct his faults.

Keep Up the Standards

So the Crew Leader, who is responsible for the appearance of his Crew, must find ways and means to keep the standards. Usually, mental note of any laxity is made and, privately, a friendly hint is passed to the offending Sea Scout. If this fails, perhaps a special effort, a visit to the Sea Scout's home or a walk with him, seemingly by accident, will give the opportunity

A GOOD CREW

for a further talk about the matter. In rare cases, it might be well to ask an officer to help in the matter. In all cases, the appeal should be made in the name of fair-play, teamwork, pulling for the honor of the Crew and the Ship.

Most common faults found by inspecting officers are unpolished shoes, dusty or linty uniforms and insignia incorrectly worn.

If you have equipped your sea chest as suggested in an earlier chapter you will have on hand a whisk broom and a shoe polish can. The best way to assure the use of these articles is this: Without a word, and while the Crew is nearby, go quietly to the sea chest and start brushing your own uniform (which we hope it will not need!) Then polish your shoes.

Without a word being said by you, these operations will be mimicked by every man in your Crew.

Show — Don't Shout!

If you find an item of insignia misplaced, you can do this:

"Hey, Harry! Your badge is on cockeyed. What's the idea, can't you read your Manual?"

Harry will not change his badge; not until he is mighty sure that everybody will have forgotten that he got a bawling out for it.

Here's a better way:

"Hey, Harry! Your badge is lower than

mine — I'll bet I sewed mine on wrong. Let's look it up in the Manual."

Harry will change his badge before the next meeting!

White hats get dirty — of course they do. In Jim Maxson's Crew meetings, off the Ship, he often idly starts cleaning his hat — salt, water, elbow grease and sunshine — and every time he is followed by every man there!

Bud Hewitt, who is pretty handy with tools, made a wall shelf with nine cubby holes. Each one is assigned to a Crew member. Now, advancement cards, candy bars, pencils and all the "junk" usually jammed into the one pocket of the Sea Scout Uniform, is neatly racked on the shelf and Bud's Crew passes inspections one hundred per cent.

A National Flagship of the Sea Scout Fleet once had an odd item in the Yeoman's expense account: one 110-volt flat iron! For neckerchiefs — every Sea Scout wanted a chance to use that iron!

And so, the Crew Leader can find many ways in which to have his Crew looking "to the Admiral's fancy" without shouting at them. In some manner, make the correction of the fault a challenge — any young man, anywhere, will take it!

A word must be said here for the young man who cannot afford to uniform completely, or, perhaps, buy black shoes or some extra piece of equipment which your Ship has adopted such as leggings or a reefer or a suit of oilers. This man should never be "hauled before the mast." He must not be made to have to buy his way into Sea Scouting. Be sympathetic and Scouting to this man. Help him find means to earn what he still needs.

Do not forget to hold frequent drills in the art of folding and stowing the uniform. The drill itself will do much to assure the presence of correct creases and smoothed nap.

Purpose of Drills

RIGHT HAND
CLASPING LEFT
THUMB
At Ease

The inspection of the Crew does not take in the uniform only of the Sea Scout but includes his posture, his correct disposition of himself in the commands of "Attention," "At ease" and "Salute."

The best way to assure smartness in this respect is to hold frequent drills in the spirit of Requirement 9 of each Sea Scout Rank and as detailed in Chapter 15 of THE SEA SCOUT MANUAL. Those which touch posture and need no room, as in marching, can often be reviewed at the Crew meeting.

It has been often noted that the command "At ease" is confused with "Parade Rest." Note in the Manual how these differ and be sure that all your Crew react to this command in the same posture.

The Sea Scout Salute, of course, is the SCOUT Salute.

Another mark of a good officer is in the matter of holding his men at "Attention!" There are periods when Sea Scouts must.

CHAPTER VI

out of respect, stand at strict attention. The good officer will always relieve his men as quickly as possible. Men standing at "Attention" for too long have been known to faint, especially when they have not been so trained over a long period.

Sea Scout Salute

Thus, the Crew Leader, always conserves the strength and spirit of his Crew when under his direct command, by ordering:

At Ease — Sea Scouts take this position but do not move from rank.

Carry On — Sea Scouts proceed with their former occupation.

Secure — Sea Scouts put up equipment and gear and stand by for next orders.

Informal — Sea Scouts are dismissed from direct command but not excused from building or present program activity. This may also be used for the command, "Be seated," which smacks too much of a minstrel show for general use before the public.

Parade Rest

As you were — Cancels previous order, returning Sea Scouts to their former positions.

A Good Crew "Out of Uniform"

Another outward appearance of the good Crew is the way it "dresses" when not in uniform. Under such circumstances, when the Crew is in bathing trunks, or a work outfit, or stripped to the waist for a bit of "capstan walking," they must be judged

A GOOD CREW

by their behavior, their general cleanliness and by their stalwart strong bodies.

The good Crew, even here, is easily recognized — for FROM HABIT, whenever they gather as a Crew, they do and say and think exactly the same things that they do when they have on the uniform.

Perhaps, next to the correct and neat wearing of the uniform, a Crew is judged by the manner in which it conducts Sea Scout Ceremonies.

Sea Scout Ceremonies

Every Ship meeting, and every Crew meeting, is opened and closed by a short ceremony.

In the case of the Crew Meeting, the ceremony should not wholly duplicate the Ship Ceremony. In Chapter 5 of this Manual some pointers are given which should enable the Crew Leader to develop a fast, snappy ceremony for his Crew meeting.

The very simplest might merely be an opening such as repeating the Scout Oath or Law, or the Sea Promise and closing with the Scout Benediction:

"May the Great Master of all true Scouts be with us till we meet again."

A great advantage in having a Crew ceremony based on the Ship Ceremony, is that it gives every Sea Scout an opportunity to practice parts of the ceremony and thus find himself true to his Scout

Motto, Be Prepared, when he is detailed to some part of the Ship Ceremony.

The Ship Ceremony will be found, fully detailed and diagrammed in Chapter 3 of THE SEA SCOUT MANUAL. The ceremony is a minimum ceremony, that is, all Ships and Patrols should regard it as required. The purpose of this standardization is that visiting Sea Scouts and Sea Scouters will feel at home on any Sea Scout Ship they board and will never be embarrassed by making a breach which will upset the host or discomfort themselves.

Many Ships, and yours might be one, have added fine salty and Scouting twists to the standard ceremony. This is in no way frowned upon and is to be encouraged providing only that the basic ceremony remains the same.

Six Important "NEVERS"

Here are a few "Nevers" which the wise officer and the Crew Leader will regard so that the solemnity of any ceremony will not be spoiled either for the Sea Scouts taking part or for the watchers:

NEVER let yourself or your Crew, by word or deed, ever suspect that you are not *actually* on shipboard.

NEVER talk or speak, except as required by the ceremony, to any man in the ranks.

NEVER permit yourself to conduct yourself except as you expect your Crew mates to conduct themselves.

NEVER attempt individualism during

A GOOD CREW 111

ceremony. You are serving, not being served!

NEVER adjust uniform or clothing; most certainly never chew gum or munch during ceremony.

NEVER be anything but courteous, considerate and gentlemanly — and this might well be applied to the entire meeting and life itself.

The Crew Leader should remember that at times he is merely a cog in a piece of complicated machinery and the failure to function properly and correctly will throw the entire machine out of gear. The officers senior to you expect your cooperation and strict attention just as you expect these things from the Sea Scouts junior to you. You are one of those extra fingers of the Skipper. He has the right to use you whenever and wherever he wishes.

Only in this way, will ceremony be smooth and a thing of vast pride and satisfaction to yourself and your Crew.

Read most carefully all the material on ceremony and visualize yourself carrying it out meticulously.

For your help and for the honor of your Crew and Ship, we append some tried and true "tricks" for the smooth conduct of Sea Scout Ceremony.

General Hints on Ceremonies

1. Detail for prominent parts in the ceremony (Color Guards, side boys, etc.) only Sea Scouts who are correctly uniformed and understand their jobs.

CHAPTER VI

2. Give your orders in clear, but not loud, conversational tones. The drill master manner is not required in Sea Scouting.

3. Do not discriminate against rank — the Apprentice can and should represent your Crew in ceremony as well as the Able Sea Scout.

4. Correct faults of your Crew members around the Crew table — *not* during ceremony.

5. Guard carefully against such natural expressions as "Hey!" and "Fellers." The ceremony gives even the correct words of address and reply.

6. Avoid touching a Sea Scout for any purpose whatsoever. In detailing a man to some duty, it is not necessary to point at him or slap him on the shoulder.

7. Squelch utterly, any giggling or laughter unless something FUNNY has occurred. Even then, it is far better to ignore the happening for the time being so that the ceremony can proceed without *mental* interruption.

Color Guards

Two men are always sent to man the ensign. One handles the halyards, the other The Flag itself, being careful that it does not at any time touch the floor. The wise Crew Leader will always personally check the halyards before the meeting so that there will be no delay by fouling when the Ship is at attention and the bugler is ready to sound off "To The Colors."

As soon as these men have their hands

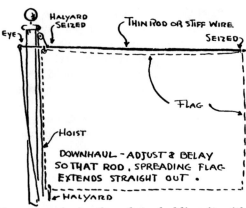

HALYARD SEIZED

EYE

THIN ROD OR STIFF WIRE

SEIZED

FLAG

HOIST

DOWNHAUL - ADJUST & BELAY SO THAT ROD, SPREADING FLAG EXTENDS STRAIGHT OUT .

HALYARD

TENNIS BALL
SPIKE
TRUCK
AWNING BLOCK

BRAIDED LINE (WILL NOT TWIST)

SNAP HOOKS

CLEAT

34"

CONCRETE CAST IN CAN OR BOX

A
GOOD FLAG STAFF
FOR THE
LAND SHIP.

free, they instantly salute, holding it with the Ship until the command "two!" They remain at attention, *at the flagstaffs,* until the command "Color Guards, return to your Crews!"

Nothing spoils the Sea Scout Closing Ceremony more than to have the Color Guard fumble about stowing The Flag at the lowering. This is a hallowed sacred moment; the Skipper has, in his Skipper's Minute, spoken from his heart and mind to you. You have been reminded of your solemn oath by repeating the Scout Oath or Law or Sea Promise and then you turn to pay your respects to The Flag of our Country. Your heart is in the solemn salute you make it — and then The Flag is sent down in a lubberly manner. No, don't let that happen. Have your color guard well trained and on its toes.

Nothing is needed to correct this fault, too often seen in the finest of Ships, except frequent practice in the Crew Meeting.

CHAPTER VI

The illustration here shows the correct and only way to fold The Flag. The sketch suggests the use of snap hooks on the halyards, rather than using a sheet bend or bowline, as this will speed up the maneuver.

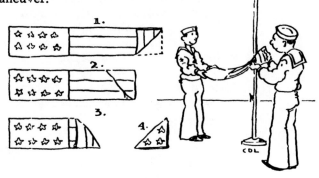

Bugler

The calls which a Sea Scout Bugler needs for the Sea Scout Ceremony are:

Assembly — At mustering before the opening, often given from the deck, the Bugler standing just forward of amidships and facing aft.

To The Colors —When raising The Flag, facing The Flag.

Retreat —When lowering The Flag, facing The Flag.

Mess Call is sometimes used to indicate dessert, a game or a special gathering, or to be told of a surprise.

Crew Leaders should instruct the Bugler to warm his mouthpiece before use so that no trumpeting will occur. Sometimes, the bugle call will be too long and greatly

A GOOD CREW 115

overlap the time of The Color raising or lowering maneuver. In this event, avoid the mistake of allowing the moment to dull by instructing the Bugler to cut the call short; or, not to repeat it several times as some bugle calls are written.

Bugle shined, lanyards clean and neat and a place for the bugle at all times (sometimes on a hook at the base of the mainmast) goes without saying.

The bo's'n's whistle may be used in place of the bugle, using the proper calls appearing later in this chapter.

Side Boys

Their duties are clearly outlined in the standard Sea Scout Ceremony. It is smart and salty for them to salute with eyes straight ahead and "unseeing." Under no circumstances are the side boys to utter a word of greeting as the visitor boards. The salute is given promptly upon the first note of the whistle and dropped with the last note. If it is necessary for the Bo's'n to stop for breath, as might be the case as a large party boards, the side boys do not drop the salute until the last man has boarded and the whistle has completed its last call.

A manner of side boys proceeding to their posts should be carefully worked out to best suit your landship layout so that no confusion takes place. This is sometimes worked out by side boys taking their posts by number. Number one advances, number two counts ten and only then advances,

I QUIT!

PR-R-OW!
OINK! ♪

numbers three to six similarly. The Bo's'n takes his place last, standing behind, that is forward, of the most inboard forward side boy. He immediately readies his whistle, bringing it to his lips as the boarding party approaches. The Bo's'n, the call finished, stands at attention, after quickly pocketing his pipe and is dismissed with the side boys at the command "Side boys, return to your Crews."

Inboard side boys return first, often using a similar number-count ten system for the maneuver as in taking positions.

Messenger Service — Special Duty

If there is need to assign a special duty to a Sea Scout the man selected for the billet is spoken to directly by the Crew Leader (who has been given the order by the Mate or the Officer of the Deck), addressing him by his rank and last name. The order is then given, briefly and concisely. The detailed man is given an opportunity to ask a question (pause for three seconds) then told to "Carry on." He replies, saluting (and the salute is smartly returned) "Aye, aye, sir!" (I have heard and understand, Sir) and carries out the order.

He reports back to the *man who gave him the order* unless otherwise instructed.

A GOOD CREW

If he carries a verbal message he salutes and, being careful not to "barge in" on a conversation or activity; says, "Skipper Jones' respects, sir. He would be honored to have you board his ship when you are ready, sir." The person for whom the message is intended will reply, opening with, "My compliments to Skipper Jones — etc." These compliments are carried by the messenger who delivers the reply opening with, "Compliments of Commodore Smith — etc."

Inspection

When inspection is indicated and the Skipper and his officers approach the Crew, the Crew Leader will at once bring his Crew to "Attention," holding them so during the inspection.

The Skipper will perhaps shake hands with the Crew Leader, after the exchange of salutes and invite him to accompany him in his inspection of the Crew. In a courteous and respectful manner give the Skipper any information he may request but be careful not to offer suggestions of your own nor air any ideas or complaints.

Upon the completion of his rounds (and if the Skipper has so requested, the rank may be ordered to, "One step forward. March!" and be returned by the command, "One step rear. March!") the Crew Leader may thank the Skipper for his inspection, will salute him as he leaves for the next Crew and immediately place his Crew "At ease."

CHAPTER VI

Under no circumstances is the Crew Leader to discuss here any Ship or Crew business with either the officers or the Sea Scouts.

Officer of the Deck

The duties of this officer so nearly approach those of the Mate, that prospective Officers of the Deck are referred to THE SEA SCOUT MANUAL on their place in ceremony. The HANDBOOK FOR SKIPPERS also gives many valuable pointers.

It is to be remembered that during his appointment, the Officer of the Deck is a full and responsible officer of the Ship. In addition to his routine duties he keeps the Harbor Log during his watch, is responsible for the physical aspects of the meeting place, its cleanliness and safety and is expected to strike, or have another Sea Scout strike, the proper half-hourly ship's bells.

These are all small things, Bo's'n, but they are the things, the little polishings and niceties, which go to make Flagships.

Be on the alert for anything which spoils ceremony for YOU. Be sure that this thing is also spoiling it for others. Then, do something about it. And, remember, that there is no place better to correct faults and develop the new ideas which will keep Sea Scouting always modern and alive, than right in the Crew.

Build Crew Spirit, so that it will build Ship Spirit and be there for all to see and feel in these two important evidences of

A GOOD CREW 119

real Sea Scouting — correct uniforming and correct ceremony.

Other Ceremonies

Many Ships have developed fine ceremonies for the induction of Apprentices, or recruits, or the celebration of advancement and achievement.

A fine Apprentice Investiture Ceremony taken from the records of the famous S.S.S. Kansan is given in the HANDBOOK FOR SKIPPERS gives the details of the cere-

A fine ceremony for the graduation of a Scout to a Sea Scout Patrol or Ship, in the same chapter, was developed by Troop 29, of Toledo, Ohio.

The Sea Scout Bridge of Honor has become famous as one of Sea Scouting's finest traditions. Chapter X of the HANDBOOK FOR SKIPPERS gives the details of the ceremony and Chapter 3 of THE SEA SCOUT MANUAL gives more.

Ceremonies, often to be held within the Crew, with other Crews as guests, might be developed for such occasions as:

Advancement (not at the Bridge or Court of Honor).

Troop Advancement of a Sea Scout.

Awards of the Red Cross.

Graduation of a Sea Scout to registered Leadership.

First appearance of a Sea Scout in uniform.

Presenting a Sea Scout project to the Troop or Pack.

Commissioning of an Emergency Service

CHAPTER VI

Corps. (See page 185.)

The return of the members from a Long
  Cruise.   .

Ceremony Develops Spirit

Any kind of ceremony, carried out with
dignity and purpose, builds spirit. Ceremony usually requires an audience to make
it real and much careful thought of properties, lighting atmosphere and "stage."
Be particularly careful not to let ceremonies such as listed become bogged down
in mere speech-making, not to embarrass
any one taking part by lavish and insin-
cere praise or by too slighting attention.
By all means, make it a matter for the
staff. Ten heads are always better than
one.

In closing this chapter, let us take a
quick survey of just how YOU, the Crew
Leader, can best contribute to this matter
of "HOW TO HAVE A GOOD CREW."

Number One, is, of course, absolute cooperation with your Ship's Officers and
Council policy.

One for All, and All for One — that
grand old motto of the ancient musketeers,
is still one that fits nobly into Sea Scouting.

Number Two is this matter of absolutely
correct and intelligent wearing and use of
the Sea Scout Uniform, its insignia and
accessories.

Number Three is to develop and maintain that healthy balance of respect,
brotherhood, "buddy-ship," and regard

A GOOD CREW

which the real leader must have to remain a leader; to be followed by others in heart and mind and deed.

Number Four is to know, without hesitation or stumbling, all that you expect your followers to know; to back up with your fullest abilities everything they do and say in ceremony and other program activities.

To make your part in Ceremony complete, to enable you to create the atmosphere of real shipboard life, the following material on the proper use of the Bo's'n's pipe is included.

The Boatswain's Call

In the Fifth Century, B.C., the Grecian Navy was rising to fame. Those naval ships were ships that were manned by large numbers of men in the rowing galley. A chief difficulty was to see that the men rowed in unison and the only way this could be done was to have some signal that all the men could hear all over the ship.

The instrument used in the Greek Navy was the flute, or whistle and the man at the oars knew exactly what to do at each sound of this flute or whistle. So far as we know this was the method used later in the Roman Navy and in all other navies up to the time of Christ.

Curiously enough, from the fall of the Roman Empire and all through the dark ages, very little is known of the history of this flute or whistle.

CHAPTER VI

During the reign of Edward I of England, from 1272 on, it is stated that the man in charge of the rowers gave signals for each stroke of the oar with the whistle.

The next clear reference to the whistle is mentioned in 1417 where a record is found that Stephen Thomas, Master of His Majesty's Ship "Trinity Royal" bequeathed his whistle to his successor Thomas Cheese.

During the next hundred years this whistle increased in importance because the next clear record made of it is in 1513 when the Lord High Admiral of the British Fleet, Sir Edward Howard received a gold whistle and jeweled gold chain from the Queen in recognition of his victory in the attack on the galleons of France in Brest. It was called the Whistle of Command and the wearer was recognized as having a special commission from the Sovereign of the country.

From then on it came to be the mark of the Admiral of the Fleet.

In 1532 Henry VIII decreed it the mark of the master of a vessel. The law was actually written this way — "Master of the ship, or other vessel, shall wear a whistle of silver with a chain of silver to hang same upon."

As the ships grew larger, the silver whistle was worn by the Mates, and as the ships became still larger it was worn by the Boatswain's Mate and still is in all the Navies in the World.

Although it has lost its designation in the Navy of being the whistle of command

and worn by the commander, it is now recognized as the instrument by which the orders of the commander are passed to the crew.

It has become so much the mark of a Boatswain that when the Boatswain is buried the whistle and lanyard are always placed on the coffin in the funeral procession.

One of the interesting stories told of this instrument concerns a parrot on board a Navy ship who could imitate the instrument. The extract, written by a man on the ship follows, "the exactness with which the bird had learned to imitate the *calls* of the Boatswain's *whistle* was uncanny. Sometimes the parrot would *pipe* an order so clearly and correctly as to throw the Ship into momentary confusion."

Note the fact that the "calls" are "piped" on the "whistle." In other words the *whistle* is the instrument, the *calls* are the signals on the instrument and the *piping* is the act of blowing the whistle.

In the Navy today, the whistle is known either as the Boatswain's Pipe, or the Boatswain's Call. The most common name for it is the Boatswain's Pipe.

So it is because of the antiquity and long tradition of the Boatswain's Pipe as a mark of leadership that in Sea Scouting we have adopted this instrument as the distinguishing mark of a Crew Leader.

Crew Leader Pipes the Call

The Skipper or the Mate gives his or-

CHAPTER VI

ders verbally to the Crew Leader who then passes the order along to his Crew either verbally or under certain circumstances by piping one of their calls.

The Crew Leader should learn to play at least the simplest of the calls and use the pipe to pass along orders wherever possible. It is salty and nautical and introduces a note of realism into Sea Scout ceremonies appreciated by both the Sea Scouts and the public. The Crew might very well receive instructions from the Crew Leader so that it will instantly recognize certain calls and might also adopt for itself a distinctive "Crew Call" to serve as a rallying signal, very much in the same manner that the Scoutmaster uses his whistle in outdoor Scout gatherings.

Tuning

It is very seldom that the Bo's'n's call can be used without tuning. Sometimes they are not shrill enough in sound and need to be adjusted to obtain the shrill note required in most of the pipes used. This is done by adjusting the pea, by flattening or soldering the sides so as to fill the space between it and the bowl. Sometimes a call can be improved by scraping the wind edge or by enlarging the hole in the bowl by filing. It is essential that the reed strikes the hole fair. This can be tested by pushing a broom straw through the reed, adjusting the wind edge until it will split the straw.

The call, after tuning, if held with its

mouth to a gentle breeze and, when blown with open hand, should sound from the most repressed pressure to the full strength of the lungs without flaw. With the hand closed the call should sound clear and shrill.

Positions of the Hand

1. There are four positions of the hand; open, curved, closed, and clinched.

2. These positions also indicate the lung force or pressure of blowing. As a rule the open hand calls for the least pressure required to make a soft, clear note; while the clinched calls for all the pressure possible to make the note shrill and clear.

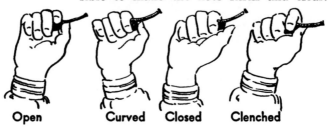

Open   Curved   Closed   Clinched

PIPING AND PASSING THE WORD

The Score, Explanation

1. The four positions of the hand—open, curved, closed, and clinched—are indicated on the four spaces of a musical staff, thus:

Clinched

Closed

Curved

Open

A. A straight line indicates a smooth note.

     CHAPTER VI

B. A dotted line indicates a rattled note.

C. A broken line indicates an undulating note.

E. Half arrowheads along a line indicate gentle breath impulses.

F. Intervals, or rests, are marked thus | with the numeral of the seconds above if more than one second is necessary, otherwise notes are slurred smoothly.

G. The number of seconds each pipe should be given under normal conditions is marked above the bar, but circumstances often call for the signal to be shortened.

2. A. Smooth notes are made as any ordinary whistle is blown, and simply raised or lowered by the lung force used.

B. Rattled notes are made by the ballarding of the tip of the tongue against the roof of the mouth, imitating a whistle rattled by a pea.

C. Undulating notes are made by a combination of the tongue slightly undulating while the throat checks the lung pressure or flow of breath, causing the sound to undulate smoothly, but continuously, at equal intervals.

Use of the Voice in Passing the Word

The tone of voice in passing the word should be modulated and pitched as the occasion calls for. The rising inflection should be given to such calls as "All hands," "Up all hammocks," etc., and the lowering inflection should be given to such calls as "Down all bags," "All the watch," etc.

Call Mates

	1	½	1
Clinched			
Closed			
Curved			
Open			

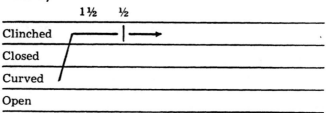

Piped by the ship's boatswain to assemble his mates.

A. Call in clinched position and sound as "peep peep," "peep peep," short and shrill with a pause of less than one second after the first two peeps.

B. This is answered by all the mates as they close on the point of assembling to receive the order to be passed from the boatswain or his chief mate, who blew the signal.

Stand By

	1½	½
Clinched		
Closed		
Curved		
Open		

Piped for "Set taut," "Stand by," and "Lay in."

Commence with call in curved position, instantly change to clinch, causing a rising peep, and follow with a slurred peep, short and ending sharp.

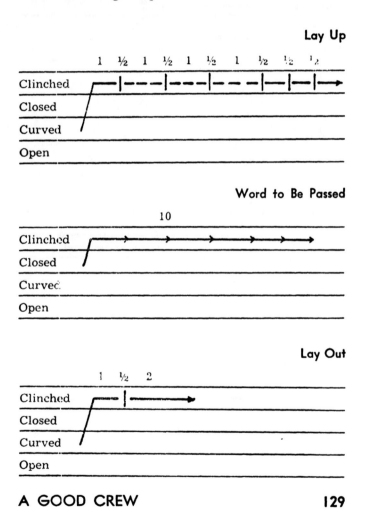

A GOOD CREW

Haul

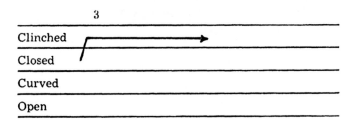

Belay

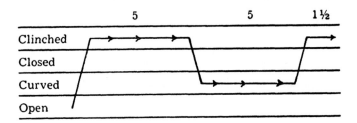

All Hands

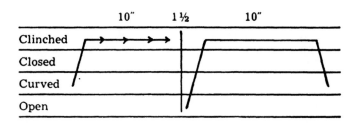

CHAPTER VI

Boat Call

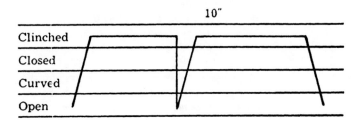

Veer

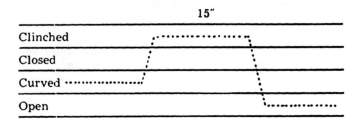

Sweepers

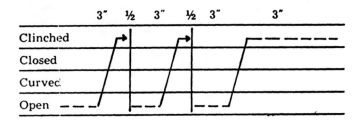

Pipe Down

A. This **pipe** is a combination of the pipe "Word to be passed" and a long veer of about 10 seconds; ending in a sharp, short peep, with an interval of one second between the two pipes.

B. This signals the termination of all evolutions and ceremonies to which all hands had been called, and is blown by the boatswain's mate of the watch. After taps, follow "Pipe down" with "Silence fore and aft."

Pipe to Meals

A. Pipe "All hands," long "Heave around" (mess gear) and long "Pipe down."

B. The combined calls should cover an interval of not less than one minute.

The call most used by Sea Scouts is the following:

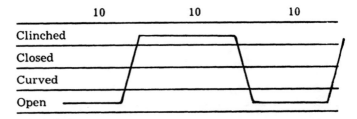

It is **blown long or short**, depending upon the time estimated for the boarding party to clear the side. Officers hold their salute until the pipe has ceased at the distinct "hook" at the very end.

CHAPTER VI

HOW TO MAKE A BOSON'S WHISTLE

THE BOWL

Discard this half

SPLIT 2 HARNESS BELLS APART. BORE A CLEAN HOLE IN ONE. USING "LIQUID SOLDER" AND A MATCH, FASTEN BOTH "GOOD" HALVES TOGETHER.

THE REED.

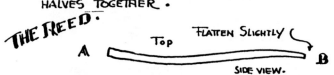

A   Top   FLATTEN SLIGHTLY   B

SIDE VIEW.

BEND A PIECE OF GASOLINE TUBING (ABOUT 1/8" I.D.) TO THE EXACT SHAPE ABOVE. SMOOTH OFF WITH A FILE AND POLISH.

THE MOUTH.

SHAPE A BONE BUTTON TO FIT SNUGLY OVER END "A" OF THE REED.

THE COMPLETED PIPE.

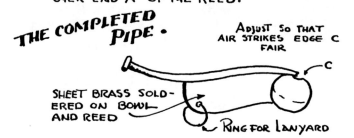

ADJUST SO THAT AIR STRIKES EDGE C FAIR

C

SHEET BRASS SOLDERED ON BOWL AND REED

RING FOR LANYARD

A GOOD CREW   133

The drawings here and on the preceding page show how to make a boat call and lanyard. A knowledge of soldering is essential. Tuning is best accomplished by the trial and error method. Such a pipe is not a show piece but will serve, lacking the Sea Scout Pipe.   .

A LANYARD
for the
WHISTLE .

FOR DRESS

FOR WORK

MAKE A 3-STRAND BRAID OF HEAVY FISH LINE .

VARYING COLORS — AN IDEA!

PURCHASE 2 YARDS OF WHITE SILK CORD AT SHADE OR UPHOLSTERY SHOP — SPLICE ENDS OVER OLD "SHOE EYES" THUS—

SERVE WITH SILK THREAD .

EYE OF WHISTLE

1. 2. 3. RING—

MAKE INTO LOOP AND ATTACH TO WHISTLE RING— THUS—

CHAPTER VII

SEA
SCOUT
ADVANCEMENT

IN the matter of prepara-
tion for Sea Scout Advancement the Crew
Leader alone has the time to give to the
individual Sea Scout all the attention and
instruction needed. The pursuit of the
knowledge and practice necessary to complete the requirements form a large and
important part of the program in both
Ship and Crew.

These requirements are so built that
while they actually go far in teaching seamanship, they also build character and
train in citizenship which, as you have
been shown, is the objective of the Scout
movement. Not all the Sea Scouts whom
you instruct will become adept at the art
of seamanship any more than they would
all become printers or lawyers if you so
instructed them. And this matters not in
the least. As long as the Sea Scout has met
the requirements squarely, has demonstrated the will to learn, has been fair
and honest and a good sport — the requirements have achieved their aim.

135

Interpretation of Requirements

The Crew Leader's approach to the Sea Scout Requirements should always be that the requirements, as printed, are minimum requirements. It is the spirit of them, that not only the letter of the printed words be observed, but that the subject be fully and thoroughly gone into. Thus the requirement under Boat Maintenance reads, "Make a sea bag or ditty bag, demonstrating the use of the flat seam, round seam and grommet eye sewed in canvas." This is relatively simple and is but a scratch on the subject of boat maintenance. The complete chapter on Boat Maintenance in THE SEA SCOUT MANUAL should be studied. The Board of Review will ask many questions and the Sea Scout wants to be thoroughly acquainted with the subject. Mere presentation of the sea bag or ditty bag is not the intention nor the spirit of this requirement.

The Crew Leader often is given the right to instruct the members of his Crew and to certify to the Skipper that he believes them thoroughly instructed and acquainted with the subject.

The Crew Leader who does this carelessly, or with a show of favoritism is the worst enemy the Crew can have. Just as surely as whales spout, the Board of Review will catch up with such tactics to the embarrassment of both the Sea Scout and the instructor.

The way to master the Sea Scout requirements is to make a thorough and

CHAPTER VII

systematic study of them, using all the program helps of the many Sea Scout and Scout books and pamphlets. The result will not be dry reading or boning or hard work -- but fun and games and activities that teach and instruct — that SHOW how not TELL how!

Would you want the responsibility of sending on a cruise the Sea Scout whom you had carelessly certified as a swimmer?

You would not, Bo's'n, nor would your officers, nor the Council.

So, in every case, back up the letter of the requirement with the spirit of the requirement.

Crew Advancement Program

In addition to the Ship Program, which will be built about Sea Scout Advancement, the Crew will also have its own advancement program.

The Crew Leader has many teaching methods at his command. None of them will do the job completely in the few hours spent weekly at the Sea Scout meeting. There must be home reading of THE SEA SCOUT MANUAL; home practice of the requirements; or off-Ship Crew meetings at which these things are done or, better yet, BOTH.

At the actual Crew Meeting, the Crew Leader can use some or all of these methods.

Reading aloud.

Discussion of an assigned section of THE SEA SCOUT MANUAL.

ADVANCEMENT 137

Presentation of the subject by experts.

Demonstration and drill.

Project and craftsmanship work.

Drawing (by the Sea Scouts or by himself on a blackboard).

Teaching by games and competition. The play-way of teaching.

Reading aloud is the lazy teacher's way of doing things. Certainly, there is nothing thrilling nor dramatic about listening to the leader stumble through pages of text. Discussion is fair, if it can be kept on the subject. And, shipmates, that takes an old experienced hand at handling classes. Presentation by experts, such as Coast Guardsmen, Red Cross officers or seamen is fine once in a while. Use such a visit as an occasion, a treat — and invite other Crews.

Demonstration and drill is perfect. It is action and each man is definitely concerned. He has a part and his sense of teamwork and natural desire to do things will be brought forward. This is also true of project work and drawing. In games and competitions, we have the same but added to it is the desire to do it better than the other man.

Work Out-of-Doors

Of course, many of the requirements are to be studied and achieved away from the Ship. These, such as cruising, cooking or swimming, can be made the reason for a Crew party or cruise or camping trip. A good rule to remember is never to try to qualify for any requirement indoors which can be qualified for on the water or in the water. Sea Scouting, like Scouting, is an outdoor program. Even in winter, when too many Ships hibernate, stifling the grand study of "sailoring" in steam-heated meeting rooms, the ingenious and imaginative Crew Leader can evolve ways and means of moving the program out-of-doors.

In some subject, some Sea Scouts, will need individual instruction and help. The Crew Leader should stand ready to give freely of his time and experience in such cases. All young men do not learn quickly. But they all *want* to learn.

In no case should the laggard be ridiculed. Work with him carefully and show a sincere interest in his problems. He'll soon catch on and surprise you. Make fun of him — and he will show his resentment by doing nothing to help his Crew.

It generally is a poor thing to instruct, then ask a few questions and sign the Sea Scout's card. Better let the information and knowledge lie a while, tying it up with other phases of seamanship later on or holding a review.

How to Examine

Written and oral examinations are necessary to qualify for some of the requirements, of course. By far the best method of examining is either by demonstrations or by project work. That is showing, not telling.

ADVANCEMENT   139

The Sea Scout who has rowed a boat has shown his mastery of the subject beyond all doubt. The one who merely tells how to do it is still one to watch when he takes out a boat.

The Sea Scout who has read material on the subject in order to draw the rigging of a brig correctly, or made a model sea anchor, or built a pelorus, understands his subjects better than a Sea Scout who merely explains it to his examiner. And, Bo's'n, it's decidedly more fun for your mates this way — and no Sea Scout Leader ever forgets that Sea Scouting is a program of FUN.

Judging Handiwork

A fine polished sloop model, neatly executed with the name and port of hail all beautifully lettered may look fine. But unless it is accurate in rigging and canvassing and deck appointments, it merely denotes a mechanical ability on the part

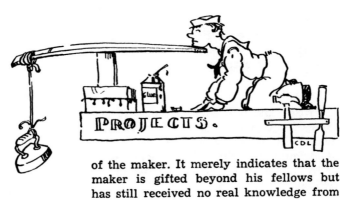

of the maker. It merely indicates that the maker is gifted beyond his fellows but has still received no real knowledge from his Sea Scouting and that knowledge is essential.

A poor looking model may be the very one that best demonstrates a mastery of the subject. Examiners are cautioned not to slight the model which admittedly is poor workmanship. It may contain the best example of what is being taught.

Of course, there are certain standards which all young men can keep up, even if not mechanically gifted. Thus, the sea bag which is dirty or paint-smeared is hardly acceptable. The cruise-log, complete with samples of the shipboard menu and cookie's jam on page two, is not in the spirit of the requirement.

Always look for neatness and evidence of the study behind the project. Give praise for the mechanically perfect but do not give blame if you know that the project has been done as well as it could be by that particular Sea Scout.

Do not forget that many of these models, projects, etc., will make fine Ship and Crew exhibits as well as serve as inspirations for the scores of Sea Scouts who will follow. By all means, arrange for their permanent exhibition.

Many of the Sea Scout Requirements might be put into project form by an imaginative examiner. Thus, the study of rope and knots might well be shown by the making of a knotboard, not now required. Sea History might be made the subject of short essays or compositions. Navigation might include a board of buoys or a light-

ADVANCEMENT

house or a model direction finder. In all cases, such additions to the requirements

A POOR SEAMAN

must be elective and done voluntarily. *No Ship may in any way alter or especially interpret the National Requirements.*

Judging Demonstration of Seamanship

Generally speaking, the teacher or examiner should know more than the student being taught or examined. This is especially true of the subject of Seamanship. If you, because of experience or long Sea Scout tenure, honestly believe that you know seamanship well, you are qualified to judge.

In any demonstration of a nautical nature, the basis of judging should most emphatically take into consideration not only the immediate subject but all that has gone before. The man who can splice one hundred per cent is NOT a seaman; he is a splicer. The man who understands

CHAPTER VII

rope, its strength and uses, and, as Davy Shellback says, "knows all about it;" who can reef, cast knots, anchor; who can use his knowledge of splicing in practical ways, is perhaps a seaman, or at least, more nearly approaching one.

For example Able Requirement No. 2 requires the Sea Scout to handle a small boat under sail. He may do this successfully, tacking, running, reaching, luffing, etc., but the careful examiner, though the requirement says nothing about this part, will also take into consideration the manner in which he has conducted himself from the moment he entered the boat until the moment he leaves her. The former training of this Sea Scout has taught him how to anchor, reef and navigate; has given him the rules of the road, chart

A GOOD SEAMAN

reading and boat etiquette. Most certainly, his present demonstration should include doing these things correctly, for only then will he have demonstrated that he is actually learning seamanship.

The Sea Scout who sails a perfect course and then makes a clumsy furl or throws a lubberly hitch on the Sampson post is hardly to be rated a seaman.

Safety a Deciding Factor

The sea is a stern master, ever ready to seize the unwary. It is the absolute duty of every examiner on or in the water to make safety a large factor in deciding whether or not the demonstration has been given in a satisfactory manner.

The handbook, SWIMMING, WATER SPORTS AND SAFETY published by the Boy Scouts of America should be in the kit of every Crew. It should be well thumbed. In it every phase of water safety from wading to boat sailing is touched. Chapter 18 of THE SEA SCOUT MANUAL contains more safety material applicable to the kind of boats which Sea Scouts are apt to use. The wise Crew Leader calls in expert adult help when it comes to rating his Crew mates as proficient watermen or seamen.

THE SEA SCOUT REQUIREMENTS — HOW TO TEACH THEM

APPRENTICE REQUIREMENTS

No. I Registration and Age:

The Quarterdeck will check this with Troop and Council records and standards.

No. 2 Scout Oath and Law:

The Crew Leader is duty bound to make these a part of the Crew program as well as his life. The best way to teach them is to live them.

No. 3 Sea Promise:

As above. Correlate this with safety, First Aid, and sea tradition.

No. 4 Safety Rules:

Home reading, Crew discussion, demonstration at waterfront or camp. Dramatize story of Titanic and the ice patrol.

No. 5 Rope:

Play rope games. Visit a rope walk, fishing vessel or ship chandlery. Know when to use the knots required. Construct knot panels for competition.

No. 6 Sea Scout Uniform:

Ownership. Insignia Chart in Crew room. Demonstration of care and folding uniforms. Visit Troop and Pack for Scouter Uniforms, listing ranks observed.

No. 7 Customs of the Sea:

Home reading. Sea fiction read at Crew meetings. Discussion. Quiz on "Glossary of Sea Terms." Dramatize a Davy Shellback yarn. As a Crew, attend a sea movie.

No. 8 Application:

Yeoman duty. Hold an investiture or graduation ceremony. Inspirational talk by prominent Scouter, pastor or educator.

ADVANCEMENT

ORDINARY REQUIREMENTS

No. 1 Sea History:

Read Part I, THE SEA SCOUT MANUAL. Practice in Crew. Sea-term quiz.

No. 2 Boats and Boat Handling:

Read. Make a scrapbook of vessel types. Visit a Coast Guard station or yacht yard. Make a model. Make a drawing. Waterfront practice. Rowing race.

No. 3 Marlinspike Seamanship:

Practice. Games. Knotboard competition. Visit a rope walk. Send for cordage catalogues. Help rig the Ship's boat.

No. 4 Rigging:

Model building. Hold model exhibit in a store window. Home reading. Invite an "old salt" to talk on sailing days. Enter commercial model contest, using a kit. Hold model boat races.

No. 5 Ground Tackle:

Make model. Read. Discuss. Demonstration of anchoring. Visit a vessel; talk with second mate, see anchoring gear, winches.

No. 6 Piloting:

Read. Study. Practice. Relative bearings game. Play Sea Scout game, Chapter 20, THE SEA SCOUT MANUAL. Send for pilot rules (any District Customs House, free). Crew sail with yachtsman. Play "Sail-O."

No. 7 Navigation:

Demonstrate with globe. Draw on white

rubber ball. Study atlas, ocean chart.

No. 8 Bridge and Quarterdeck:

Practice. Practice. Practice. Talk by a signal or radio expert. Keep bell time in Crew meetings. Visit a busy harbor, logging all flags seen.

No. 9 Drill:

Frequent drill practice. Council approved participation in parades.

No. 10 Swimming:

Merit Badge standards to be attained. Swim often for fun. Observe laws of safety. Read history of swimming, Chapter I of "SWIMMING, WATER SPORTS AND SAFETY."

No. 11 Boat Maintenance:

Project. Read. Survey Ship's boat and estimate needed work. Visit by sailmaker. Watch a yacht being fitted out.

No. 12 Cruising:

Overnight cruise. Require Sea Scouts to demonstrate in practical ways all they have so far learned. Make MANY cruises. Pass this requirement ten times a year!

No. 13 Safety:

Ship drills. Adopt a Billet system. *Tie up safety with requirements you present.* Demonstrate rescue work. Visit harbor police base or Coast Guard station. Hold safety drill with another Ship.

No. 14 Galley and First Aid:

Demonstration at camp, hike or cruise. Hold cooking and tent-raising competitions. Study COOKING Merit Badge pamphlet. Hold a father-son cruise or beach hike, Sea Scouts cooking. Visit the galley of a liner. Attend Scout Camporee.

No. 15 Service:

Service is NEVER merely time elapsed, it is what the Sea Scout has done. Let your officers judge this. Take part in Crew or Ship community service.

No. 16 Leadership:

Practice at Crew and Ship ceremonies. Play several games under candidate's leadership, take a cruise, hold a drill. Submit a Crew program for one month. Act as O.D. (or Mate) four times.

No. 17 Scout Organization:

Read. Discuss. Ask District Commissioner for a talk. See Scout movies.

THE ABLE REQUIREMENTS

No. 1 Sea History:

Read fiction or sea short stories. See appropriate movie as a Crew. Write a theme on some part of sea history. Make a chart, showing evolution of ships. Make models of primitive craft. Visit a marine museum. Talk with marine engineers, skippers or U. S. Navy men. Hold a water parade with small boats to represent ship types.

No. 2 Boats and Boat Handling:

Practice. Watch a Coast Guard surf station at practice. Hold inter-Crew races.

Arrange to be present at life boat drill required on all steam vessels. Attend a Council or Regional Regatta. Instruct candidates for Seamanship Merit Badge.

No. 3 Splicing:

Demonstration. Games, Practice. Help rig a boat. Make a model foremast, complete with rope standing rigging. Build a complete mast, properly stayed, at the Scout Camp or Sea Scout base.

No. 4 Rigging:

As above. Make model boat to sail in competition. Attend model boat regatta. Play sail game, Chapter VI, HANDBOOK FOR SKIPPERS. Build set of simple sails. Make sail cover, gaskets or reef points.

No. 5 Mooring:

Read. Practice. Sing a "Capstan-walking" chanty. (SONGS SEA SCOUTS SING.) Visit a vessel. Demonstrate in a boat. Talk by a deep-sea diver. Play "Sail-O." Send for tide tables to predict tide for your vicinity. Visit chain factory.

No. 6 Buoyage System and Rules of the Road:

Sketch or model after reading and discussion. Play "Sail-O." Visit Bureau of Lighthouses shore station (now under U. S. Coast Guard). Read fiction, including "Grace Darling." Build a model lighthouse that blinks, or a ten-foot one for the base. Demonstrate Rules of the Road with models, then actual boats (or with bicycles, or on skates).

ADVANCEMENT   149

No. 7 Navigation:

Study chart, Bowditch, Coast Pilot. Navigate any vessel, but often! Read life of Columbus — shipmates, there was a navigator! Write theme on shipping. Quiz an air-pilot on navigational aids. Hold mock crew whaler's gam.

No. 8 Signaling:

Send actual messages to make it live. Use Boy Scout signal disc. Apply a flashlight battery blinker system to your model boat. Demonstrate the submarine bell while swimming; also Morse Code by tapping stones under water. Make a real set of code flags and use. Make a heliograph (merely mirrors!) Send blinker messages.

No. 9 Drill:

Practice. Parade. Crew ceremony, to which is added commands from the School of the Crew. Drill competitions.

No. 10 Swimming:

Swimming instruction with the accent on safety and rescue work. Much practice; at pools in winter. Build problems and demonstrations for the Crew to solve.

No. 11 Boat Maintenance:

Work! Actual opportunities to put into practice all the Sea Scout has learned should be provided. Give each man some part of the equipment for which to be fully responsible. Subscribe to a yachting magazine. Competition for boat color schemes, running rigging. List stores to be carried and estimate weight. Instruction from an expert caulker or painter. Hold a ship launching party with formal commissioning.

No. 12 Cruising:

As provided by Council Standards. Preparation for this cruise might be a review of all requirements. Give it publicity. Have the picture of your Crew in the paper or the high school class book. Hold an exhibition of the logs and photos taken. Make a cruise movie. Arrange an itinerary that will meet other Ships on a cruise, or visit sister Ship Sea Scout bases.

No. 13 Safety:

Project and reading, especially old-time sea fiction. Pay a visit, or cruise, to a Coast Guard base. Make a real breeches buoy for use at Scout rallies or camporees. Dramatize a shipwreck. Send breeches-buoy instruction to a fancied wrecked ship by semaphore; by blinker; by Morse code.

No. 14 First Aid:

Merit Badge standards required. Study with the Troop. Invite District First Aid Counsellor to demonstrate. Use living models. Play First Aid games. Make a floating dummy, launch him and send Ship's boats after him. Label his arm broken, his ankle twisted and drop him from a masthead — apply First Aid!

No. 15 Service:

In chapter on, "Things for Crews to Do" are many useful civic and Ship services.

No. 16 Leadership:

> Actually practice these berths, relieving present incumbents or working as their assistants for a month's period. Detail candidate as Crew Yeoman, purser or carpenter.

No. 17 Scout Organization:

> Reading, discussion. Visit Troop, Den, Pack, Patrol, District or Council meeting. Take a hike with the Troop or Rover Crew. Sit in on a Ship's Committee meeting. Read National Council By-Laws. Dramatize a District meeting within the Crew.

QUARTERMASTER REQUIREMENTS

> Sea Scout Requirements for the rank of Quartermaster are similarly approached.
>
> Note how often the words *demonstrate* and *project* and *do* appear — and how seldom merely *read*. Every Sea Scout Requirement can be made to live, to stand out as vital and compelling and challenging. Not one of them is stale or dull. The suggestions given are not rules — merely a springboard for Crew Leaders to "take off" from and show the Movement some really fine ideas. Good luck, Bo's'n!
>
> Games will be found in the HANDBOOK FOR SKIPPERS, THE SEA SCOUT MANUAL, HANDBOOK FOR PATROL LEADERS and ADVENTURING FOR SENIOR SCOUTS.
>
> Ideas will be found, due north, behind a pair of observant eyes, in a deep cove called "The Mind."

CHAPTER VII

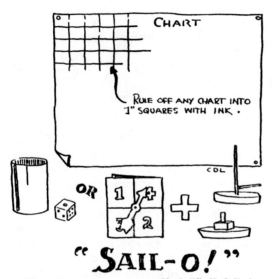

"SAIL-O!"

Here is a new game, called "Sail-O," designed especially for Sea Scouts and easily made by any live Crew. The cost will be under a dollar, (or less if you know a Davy Shellback with an old chart).

Forty-four games have been played on it each one of which TEACHES SEA SCOUTING.

The model boats, very simple, and painted red, blue, white, etc., can be an assortment of the following types:

Naval vessel	Dredge
Liner	Speed boat
Freighter	Outboard motor boat
Square Rigger	Sea Scout cruiser
Sloop-yacht	Coast Guard patrol

Each Sea Scout (and as many as eight can play) takes one boat as his own. He

moves it IN ANY DIRECTION DESIRED as many squares as indicated by the number he has spun. He moves the vessel always with the objective of the game being played in view and with due regard for channels, dangers to navigation and the limitations of the waters shown by the chart. The boat is never moved over land, nor are rules of the road violated nor the vessel (as in the case of a sailing ship) maneuvered in such a way as would be impossible.

1. Rules of the Road.

Two fleets, in port, at opposite corners of the chart must change ports. As they move they must keep clear of each other and the fleet passing them. The first fleet entirely at anchor wins.

2. The same with all vessels drawing ten feet of water. Watch the channels!

3. The same with all vessels regarded as cat boats and the wind in the northwest.

4. The same as 3, with the wind shifting at a time set by the Crew Leader to West (thus changing the sailing courses!).

5. Four steamers are racing to a drawbridge (find one on the chart). They give

CHAPTER VII

proper whistle signals to each other and to the bridge tender. First one through wins.

6. A ship is wrecked off-shore. An imaginary SOS calls all models to her rescue. First one to reach wreck is winner.

7. Same but winner must tell how he affected a boarding of the wreck.

8. Same but winner must take wreck in tow and beat the others back to a designated port.

9. Vessels race from port to port, drawing five feet. During progress a message comes by blinker (or code). Skippers must interpret message and follow the orders (they may be sent into nearest port or called to a wreck or told to anchor in a lee).

10. Vessels are proceeding seaward, when Crew Leader suddenly displays storm warnings (with model paper flags or colored beads for night signals). Each Skipper reads warning and acts to his best judgment, running for port, anchoring, etc.

11. Vessels are racing, port to an off-shore buoy. Crew Leader indicates man overboard by throwing some object on chart nearby. Vessels must make rescue, winning skipper explaining his method.

12. Same with a ship suddenly on fire.

13. Same with a ship in collision.

14. Square riggers are in grain race, making port, with wind southeast. Sudden shift of wind to other board. Skippers must make and explain new courses.

ADVANCEMENT   155

15. Two vessels race. At every third move, skippers must give the relative bearing of the other vessel.

16. Any of these games in fog, vessels giving proper fog signals.

17. Any of these games, with skipper taking and calling soundings.

18. A tug and her tow is sailing along steamship lanes. Skipper takes and explains his rights.

19. One barge at a time is dropped at predetermined ports. Skipper explains his change of lights and signals.

20. Yacht race. Rules of the road for sail prevail.

21. Outboard motor boat race, with sailboats on the course.

22. All boats sail a given compass course, changing as indicated by the Crew Leader. Courses must be correct with variation figured.

23. Boats proceed from port to port. At any time, Crew Leader may order anchors down. Skipper must explain the type anchor he used and why.

24. A bad set of tide threatens. With every move forward, the vessel must take one-square move to port (or starboard). Object is to move so that vessel is clear of dangers.

How to Use Sail-O

Any Sea Scout Requirement, or any combination, which is even better, can be made to live in these games and problems.

For example: Crew Leader: "The fleet

CHAPTER VII

is drawing near the equator. Sea Scout
Jones, what changes in uniform would you
advise? Why?"

"Sea Scout Smith, what changes in diet
are indicated? Why?"

Or this: Crew Leader: "The first vessel
within three squares of Neversink Light
report — and give a brief history of lighthouses."

Or this: "Ship's Skipper, maneuvering
his own vessel, is given the correct salutes
and rights."

Or this: "A mysterious gunboat appears
(operated by a crew of badmen!) Object,
catch it, corner it, ram it — anything
that's *fun!*"

Don't forget, Bo's'n, that Sea Scout
games are fine for examining as well as
instructing and recreation. You'll have a
much better attendance and spirit than
by merely reading or talking.

Help from the Quarterdeck

Sea Scout Advancement is carried out
under the careful guidance of the quarterdeck. Crew Leaders should understand and
explain to their Crews the National Council Standards of Advancement based on
the requirements.

When a Sea Scout has been certified as
ready to appear before the Board of Review the Crew Leader and the Ship's
Officers will make the necessary arrangements. If a Sea Scout Board of Review
does not exist in the District or Council,
the Scout Board of Review, to which may
be added some persons of nautical back-

ADVANCEMENT   157

ground, will examine the candidate. The Sea Scout is judged not only upon his knowledge and his exhibits but by his gentlemanly Scout bearing and manner.

If he successfully passes the Board of Review, he is certified by that Board to the Committee on Advancement as eligible to be advanced to the next rank and permission is granted to wear the badge of that rank. It is to be noted that Ship's Officers can not advance a Sea Scout. This is handled and authorized by the Council Committee on Advancement.

After this, the actual advancement is made at a Bridge of Honor or at a Court of Honor. The badge may or may not be given at this affair. At any rate, a certificate will be given and the Council records brought up to date.

Many Ships, wisely using the Ship Budget Plan, present the badge without additional cost to the Sea Scout at a Ship or District meeting.

Crew Leaders are encouraged to have their mates make Troop Advancement along with their Sea Scout Advancement. Sea Scouting, as shown by the chart below, leads to the Eagle Scout Rank as well as the Quartermaster Rank.

Advanced Scout Ranks

Sea Scouts are eligible to qualify for the advanced ranks of Star, Life and Eagle by meeting the same qualifying standards required for Boy Scouts. In order to aid Sea Scouts in meeting these standards, the following interpretation of Sea Scout Requirements was approved by the National Executive Board of the Boy Scouts of America in April, 1939.

SECOND CLASS

The Ordinary Sea Scout may qualify for Second Class Scout Rank if he meets these additional Second Class Requirements not covered in the work of the Ordinary Sea Scout:

First Aid

(a) *Show* what to do, including proper dressing and binder where necessary for cut on finger; knee deeply scraped and bleeding; cut on forearm; bleeding nose; blister on heel; severe scald from hot liquid or steam; black eye; fainting; shock; blow in pit of stomach; apparent death from inhaling gas; drowning or electric shock.

Tell what should and what should not be done for pimple on face; earache; splinter under fingernail; cinder in eye; sunburn. *Tell* danger of taking a physic for pain or soreness in region of stomach without first consulting a physician.

Tracking

Track half mile in twenty-five minutes; or, if in town, describe satisfactorily the contents of one store window out of four observed for one minute each.

Scout's Pace

Go a mile in twelve minutes at Scout's

Pace — about fifty steps running and fifty walking, alternately; or lay out, measure by the stride method and stake a four-acre tract of land.

Thrift

Earn and deposit at least one dollar in a public bank or other savings institution (U. S. Defense Bonds or Stamps, also premiums paid on life insurance are accepted, if earned); or earn, own and raise some farm animal; or earn and contribute at least one dollar or the equivalent to the family budget or to welfare work in the community.

FIRST CLASS

Thrift

The Able Sea Scout may qualify for First Class Scout Rank if he meets these additional First Class Requirements:

(1) First Class Thrift:
Earn and deposit at least two dollars in a public bank or other savings institution (U. S. Defense Savings Bonds or Stamps, also premiums paid on life insurance are accepted, if earned); or plant, raise, and market a farm crop, or earn and contribute at least two dollars or the equivalent to the family budget or to welfare work in the community.

Judging

Judge distance, size, number, height and weight within 25%.

Nature

Be able to identify in the field, (1a) 10 species of trees or plants, including poison ivy, noting such characteristic things as bark, leaves, flowers, fruit, and scent; or (1b) 6 species of wild birds noting such characteristics as plumage, notes, tracks and habits; or (1c) 6 species of native wild animals, noting characteristic form, color call, track and habits. (2) Be able to point out the North Star, and be able to name and point out at least 3 constellations of stars.

This interpretation of the Second Class and First Class Scout Ranks is made to aid those Sea Scouts who come into the Sea Scouting Program without previous Scout experience, or perhaps those who did not attain these ranks in their Troop experience. This enables them to qualify for Second and First Class Scout Rank through the Sea Scout Patrol or Ship.

MERIT BADGE PROGRAM

The Merit Badge Program is a part of Sea Scouting. The Crew Leader should appreciate this fact and at every opportunity encourage his Crew members to carry on their Merit Badge work.

When the Senior Scouting Program was announced in 1933, including Senior Scouting in the Troop, Explorer Scouting, Rover Scouting and Sea Scouting, strong emphasis was placed on the Senior Scout's carrying on in the Merit Badge Program. To encourage the Senior Scout to further his knowledge and skills, the National Council of the Boy Scouts of America has developed the following standards for

ADVANCEMENT   161

Senior Scout progress in special interest fields.

To qualify in the knowledge and skills represented by the Senior Scout titles the Senior Scout should meet the following requirements.

1. Select one of the fields below, and in consultation with his Skipper and the approved Merit Badge Counselors in that field.

2. Develop a plan of personal interest which will involve the securing of certain Merit Badges in that field (five is suggested as a reasonable number) and also advanced work in one or more of those Merit Badge subjects beyond the Merit Badge requirements as set forth.

3. Plan and carry out a service project in this field which involves the skills attained in meeting the requirements for the Merit Badges. This service project may be for the home, church, school, Troop, neighborhood or community.

4. Report to the Skipper and to the Ship the following:

(a) If it is a vocational field, report the preparation involved before employment can usually be secured, the general abilities an individual must have in order to succeed in the vocation, and the changes for employment at the present time. This presentation should include, either in written or oral form, an outline of the Scout's general knowledge of the field and his appreciation of what is involved in pursuing it as a life work.

(b) If it is an avocational or hobby field, report the general skills involved, the cost of materials and the general satisfaction derived from the activity.

Scout Artist

Architecture, Dramatics, Indian Lore, Landscape Gardening, Music, Painting, Pottery, Photography, Sculpture.

Scout Craftsman

Basketry, Bookbinding, Carpentry, Cement Work, Foundry Practice, Handicraft, Leathercraft, Masonry, Metal Work, Plumbing, Pottery, Printing, Woodcarving, Wood Turning, Wood Work.

Scout Artisan

Architecture, Automobiling, Aviation, Blacksmithing, Carpentry, Chemistry, Electricity, Foundry Practice, Machinery, Masonry, Rocks and Minerals, Plumbing, Radio, Safety, Surveying.

Scout Naturalist

Agriculture, Angling, Astronomy, Bee Keeping, Bird Study, Botany, First Aid to Animals, Forestry, Gardening, Indian Lore, Insect Life, Photography, Reptile Study, Stalking, Taxidermy, Zoology.

Scout Seaman

Angling, Canoeing, First Aid, Life Saving, Radio, Rowing, Seamanship, Signaling, Swimming, Weather.

Scout Sportsman

Angling, Archery, Canoeing, Conservation, Hiking, Rowing, Stalking, Swimming, Physical Development, Athletics, Skiing, Horsemanship.

Scout Woodsman

Cooking, Camping, Pioneering, Conservation, Marksmanship, Weather, Hiking, Canoeing, Forestry, Stalking, First Aid, Public Health, Personal Health.

Scout Radioman

Radio, Electricity, Signaling, Metal Work, Weather, Chemistry, Mechanical Drawing, Astronomy.

Scout Journalist

Journalism, Printing, Interpreting, Art, Photography, Dramatics, Reading, Scholarship, Salesmanship, Business.

Scout Citizen

Civics, Public Health, Personal Health, Firemanship, Public Speaking, First Aid, Pathfinding, First Aid to Animals, Safety, Conservation, Finger Printing.

The Sea Scout, before he is eligible to meet the requirements for any given Merit Badge, must have attained the Scout rank necessary for that Badge.

CHAPTER VIII

LEADERSHIP AND CITIZENSHIP

by Dr. William C. Menninger.
National Commodore's Staff.

Sometimes, perhaps, while listening to the Skipper's Minute you have been halted a moment in the daily tread to think of the future. Perhaps sometime while listening to a sermon you stopped a minute to look forward and wonder what you were going to make of yourself. Or it might have been the remarks of some close friend or one of those rare talks with dad or mother that gave you a momentary vision of what was to come.

Most of this book has been devoted to giving suggestions to you about how to run your Crew. If you have learned something from it, if you have been able to follow it, if you have given your Crew a lot of fun in the Game of Sea Scouting, you have grown a great deal yourself. But it seems desirable to add just a word about you and what your job as Crew Leader can mean for you.

Have you ever stopped to think that there are very few men, very, very few, who ever have an opportunity to direct four, six, or eight other men? Have you stopped to think that an executive with six or eight men under his direction has probably worked for a good many years to reach such a post? And yet this is your chance to do exactly that thing. So perhaps most important, much more important than any particular method that you use with your group, is the sort of fellow you make of yourself. Early in this book the suggestion was made that to set the example was probably the most important element in leadership. If you can and have succeeded in setting the example your Crew members will reflect it. Consequently as you think about the future, as you think of your responsibilities in the years to come and of how you can utilize Sea Scouting to help you in that direction, so you can direct your Crew in thinking about the same things.

What is your future? No one knows, of course. Whatever your private hopes and ambitions may be, we know full well that you are some time going to have the full responsibility of being a man, of taking a part in the community in which you live, of lending all your heart and soul to maintaining and preserving and improving the democracy of our country. In short, your Sea Scouting should furnish you an ideal opportunity to train for that big job — being a citizen.

You may rightfully ask, where can I get some concrete ideas about being a citizen, about my responsibilities for citizenship? Sea Scouts aren't satisfied, however, with generalities; they may look to you as their leader to give them some specific information, some specific challenge. By all means you ought to reread the Constitution of the United States. In fact, the whole Crew should do so. Probably the one most important brief bit of information which as a citizen you should know is what is termed *The Bill of Rights,* the term applied to the first ten Amendments to the Constitution. For your convenience they are given here.

THE BILL OF RIGHTS

Congress shall make no law respecting an establishment of religion, or prohibiting the free exercise thereof; or abridging the freedom of speech, or of the press;

or the right of the people peaceably to assemble, and to petition the government for a redress of grievances.

A well regulated militia, being necessary to the security of a free state, the right of the people to keep and bear arms shall not be infringed by law.

No soldier shall, in time of peace, be quartered in any house, without the consent of the owner; nor in time of war, but in a manner to be prescribed by law.

The right of the people to be secure in their persons, houses, papers and effects, against unreasonable searches and seizures, shall not be violated, and no warrants shall issue but upon probable cause, supported by oath or affirmation, and particularly describing the place to be searched and the persons or things to be seized.

No person shall be held to answer for a capital or otherwise infamous crime, unless on a presentment or indictment of a grand jury, except in cases arising in the land or naval forces, or in the militia when in actual service, in time of war or public danger; nor shall any person be subject for the same offense to be twice put in jeopardy of life or limb; nor shall be compelled, in any criminal case, to be a witness against himself, nor be deprived of life, liberty or property, without due process of law, nor shall private property be taken for public use without just compensation.

In all criminal prosecutions the accused shall enjoy the right to a speedy and public trial by an impartial jury of the state and district wherein the crime shall have been committed, which district shall have been previously ascertained by law, and to be informed of the nature and cause of the accusation; to be confronted with the witnesses against him; to have compulsory process for obtaining witnesses in his favor, and to have the assistance of counsel for his defence.

In suits at common law, where the value in controversy shall exceed twenty dollars, the right of trial by jury shall be preserved, and no fact tried by a jury shall be otherwise re-examined in any court of the United States than according to the rules of the common law.

Excessive bail shall not be required, nor excessive fine imposed, nor cruel and unusual punishments inflicted.

The enumeration in the constitution of certain rights, shall not be construed to deny or disparage others retained by the people.

The powers not delegated to the United States by the constitution, nor prohibited by it to the states, are reserved to the states, respectively, or to the people.

For specific challenges for you and your Sea Scouts there are countless opportunities and tasks, literally there is no limit. In our Scouting literature there are two beautiful presentations of challenges, one by our National Director of Senior Scouting, Thomas J. Keane, and one by our Chief Scout Executive, Dr. James E. West. It will pay you rich dividends to read these, to study them, to think about them, and to put them into action.

Mr. Keane's challenge deals with the presentation of the Badge of the Sea Scout Quartermaster. It applies equally well however, to every Apprentice. It follows in full:

CHALLENGE TO THE QUARTERMASTER

"The Sea Scout Quartermaster is the highest rank in Sea Scouting, and of the many who start with the hope of reaching this goal, only a few arrive. For some the difficulties have been too great — for others, circumstances have been against them. Some overcome the difficulties, use the circumstances to suit their purpose, stand steadfast towards their object and reach their goal. They are to be congratulated most heartily.

"During the years that boys are in Scouting, they are given the opportunity to learn the worth of many things, spiritual and material. They are taught how to make a choice between the things that are of real value and those of no value. This is an invaluable training. Men of high character have been happy to have been associated with them as leaders, giving them an opportunity to form their own ideals of what a man should be.

"During this time also, older Scouts have been able, through the Sea Scout Program, to learn of the sea and ships, of the great navigators and explorers who gave their lives for the advancement of human knowledge. Men who showed by their determination, daring and courage that success is within the reach of all who work hard enough to attain it.

"Before setting out on their voyages, these men were prepared. They learned to take care of themselves on the water by practicing the handling of boats and small sailing vessels around the harbors and along the shores of their native places.

"So it is with life. The adolescent has been sailing around in the harbor of life, close to the shore, protected by many sheltering influences, but he must now venture upon the great ocean of experience where he will make a long voyage. Whether he will reach the harbor on the other side will depend entirely upon himself. No shipmaster would attempt a voyage without a rudder, without a compass, without an anchor. He knows how essential these things are to the success of his passage across the sea. He knows he must have instruments to guide him. So with the Sea Scout. He, too, must be prepared and supply himself with instruments.

CITIZENSHIP   169

"The instruments that he uses, however, are spiritual as well as material, and in order to be reminded of them, he is presented with the Sea Scout Quartermaster Badge. This badge is a recognition of accomplishment in the past and a guide for him in the future. One of its essential parts is a compass card.

"Of all the things around, in, and aboard ships, the compass is the only thing that points constantly in one direction. The north point of the compass card always points to the north — a faithful guide to the navigator, who plots his course before he leaves port; sets the prow of his ship in the direction he wishes to follow and, by means of the compass, knows whether he is on his course or not.

"Scouting has taught the Sea Scout that he must plot his course if he is to complete his voyage safely and happily, and the compass that it gives him is the Scout Oath and Law, always pointing in one direction — the right one.

"Another element of this badge is the ship's wheel. In every life, as in every voyage, storms and contrary winds arise, sometimes unexpectedly. No matter how carefully a course is plotted, the ship may be driven off. The shipmaster brings his ship back on her true course by means of the wheel. A Scout's life purpose may be diverted, but like the ship, it may be brought back on the right course. The instrument he must use for this is his force of character.

"In Scouting, the leader tries to teach the boy how to develop his character in such a way that it will help him in an emergency, just as the quartermaster at sea is taught to use the wheel of his vessel to keep her on her course.

"The third part of this badge is — the anchor. Every voyage must come to an end. This end is signified by letting go of the anchor. Every life must come to an end. The anchor of this badge is a constant reminder of this. But the Supreme Skipper of the Universe has said that there is a reward for those who make their voyages well. So this anchor is an emblem of hope for them.

"The Scout Emblem, the keystone of this badge, serves to recall the three great points of the Scout Oath —

1. Duty to God and to Country
2. Duty to Others
3. Duty to Self

"If the Sea Scout Quartermaster is true to these three things, there is nothing for him to fear. He is on the threshold of a great adventure. The ship on which he is about to embark is God's greatest gift — Life. Fortified by his experience in Scouting, he can plot his course, unfurl his sails, stand by the wheel and whether the winds be fair or foul, look forward to a happy and successful voyage."

The greatest challenge given to Senior Scouts has come from our Chief Scout Executive, Dr. James E. West, in a Foreword to the book, *Adventuring for Senior Scouts*. It includes a citizenship dedication and because it so aptly applies to Crew Leaders and to their Sea Scouts a considerable portion of it is quoted in the conclusion of this Manual.

CHALLENGE FROM THE CHIEF SCOUT EXECUTIVE

"You, as Senior Scouts, not alone by age, but by special training as Scouts, have acquired a definite and distinctive citizenship standing in the scheme of things as they are today, which involves not only many pleasures and privileges, but definite responsibilities. You have accepted the personal responsibility to plan your daily life and actions so as to keep yourselves physically strong, mentally awake and morally straight! You need not wait until you reach voting age to make your influence felt as sturdy, loyal citizens. All about you, every day, are opportunities to serve and "take hold" as citizens, not alone through Scouting and its civic service, but through church, school, grange, neighborhood and other groups.

"Be constantly alert for opportunities to cooperate and render service. Cultivate your capacity to understand and care about other people. Be tolerant and respect the rights of others. Develop courage, self-reliance. Be vigilant in showing by your speech and action your faith in America, your faith in God. As Scout Citizens, accept your responsibility for extending among those with whom you come in contact their understanding and appreciation of the ideals of Scouting and the principles that have made us, and in my judgment will always keep us, a great Democracy.

"The aim of the Scout Movement has been to give you personal help in the building of your character and in training yourself for citizenship, and now you are called upon to serve as 'participating citizens.' Throughout the ages, the Athenian Oath has served a useful purpose in stirring people everywhere to better citizenship. In this spirit, I recommend for your individual consideration and voluntary action, in addition to maintaining your obligation under the Scout Oath, or Promise, and Laws, the following Senior Scout Citizenship Dedication:

"As a Senior Scout Citizen:

"1. *I will* continue to live the Scout Oath and Law.

"2. *I will* keep myself familiar with the Declaration of Independence and the Constitution of the United States — with its Bill of Rights and obligations.

"3. *I will* respect and obey the law — to further that true freedom and security for all, which comes with liberty under law.

CHAPTER VIII

"4. *I will* wholeheartedly cooperate in the responsibilities of my home, and will participate in the civic and social activities of my school, church, neighborhood and community, and, when legally qualified, I will regularly register and vote in community, state and national elections.

"5. *I will* deal fairly and kindly with my fellow citizens of whatever race or creed, in the spirit of the Twelfth Scout Law and its faith in God, and America's guarantee of religious freedom.

"6. *I will* work for America and will guard our heritage — its liberties and responsibilities — realizing that the privileges we enjoy today have come as a result of the hard work, sacrifice, faith and clear thinking of our forefathers, and I will do all in my power to transmit our America, reenforced, to the next generation.

"We place these things before you confident that you will keep the fine spirit of American reverence, tolerance and loyalty burning in your life as a 'participating citizen,' who cares about his fellow citizens and seeks to "help other people at all times." That spirit is the life blood of America. Guard it and live it!"

You have been given a trust and assumed a great responsibility. All your years in Scouting have been years of training in trustworthiness. The men who have been great have been those who were trustworthy.

And what is this trust that has been given to you? You have been selected to be the leader of a group of your comrades, a Crew of Sea Scouts.

If you guide your Crew well now, you will be given a larger Ship, a greater trust later on and in a very great measure the way in which you carry out your present trust will determine how you will carry out the greater trust later.

Everyone is pulling for you to succeed. You can, if you will!

DAVY SHELLBACK SAYS FAREWELL...

So, me Sea Scout bucko, we've come to the last page, we have. There ain't no more. Ye've been given of the helps as have made mighty Crew Leaders afore you. Ye've been readin' o' the wisdom o' seamen and leaders an' been shipmates with that grand spirit o' ships and sailormen which made America an' Sea Scoutin'.

There you be, laddy-mate, all upstandin' an' proud, wearin' yer ancient badge o' leadership, the bo's'n's whistle, an' with eight eager Sea Scouts waitin' on yer leadership. Mate, what are ye reckonin' on givin' 'em? Orders? Pipe calls? Demerits with the Skipper aft?

You can do it, Bo's'n. 'Tis yer right in a way. But the lads won't love you. They'll obey you an' salute you han'-some an' reef an' furl so's you can't report 'em aft. Old Davy knows, lad? He's seen it on a hundert great Ships like yourn, he has. The Bo's'n who ain't a mate; the Crew Leader who ain't a friend an' a pal an' a Scout.

Davy Shellback grieves on the picture, he does. The saddest and loneliest mortal on the seven oceans is him with the brains and brawn to lead his mates but not the common human ability to make himself loved an' respected. Hist to a yarn, matey . . . Davy'll spin one more, he will an' hope sincere that ye'll never ferget its moral.

Down in Rio we was, in the full-rigger OLD GLORY, a happy crew just made port an' waitin' dockin' orders. The Old Man gave us shore leave an' we skylarked in town, gammin' here an' there with old maties from other ships an' watchin' the spunky little 'pprentices hob-nob with the Spanishers. Well, sir, we was standin' in the parado, the town all gay an' color-runnin', when up tacks my skipper.

174

His kind face was anxious an' he was a'puffin' like a ironed grampus.

"Davy," me skipper sez, "Davy, you an' the boys git back to the ship quick. On the jump, bo's'n. I'll jine you immediate."

"Aye, aye, Sir," Davy sez an' pulls his forelock respeckful, "an', beggin' your kindness, Sir, what's the great rush "

"Plenty, lad," the Old Man snorts, "Don Alverez, him that governs this town, is comin' aboard for a visit. Davy, we got to turn out a full watch fer him; neat and clean and handsome."

Now, Old Davy turns to an' his whistle calls all hands an' before the sun makes a tick o' westing, we're all back on board. Mate, you ain't got no idea o' how we scrubbed and polished the vessel, nor, how, when it shined to suit a gouty Admiral, we scrubbed an' polished ourselves. Davy's watch-mates looked mighty slick an' trim, they did, fitten' to be onrecognized by the mothers as bore 'em! The other bo's'n's were turnin' their own watches out as slick; even Tom Cringle, who was one o' these unloved watch-leaders as Davy mentioned previous. Well, matey, we just had time to take our crew stations on the main deck when the fort fires 'bout forty guns an' out comes Don Alverez in his great barge.

"Very good, Davy," me skipper sez back-handed, standin' on his quarterdeck, proud an' struttin' like a peacock bird, "the ship looks grand an' the hands are sure smart."

An' then, sudden there's a roll o' drums an' the shrill cry o' the pipe, an' Don Alverez stands on the spotless deck o' our ship OLD GLORY. A fine man, mate . . . straight an' keen an' level-eyed. "A seaman hisself," Davy whispers an' stands very straight for Don Alverez was inspectin' the crews.

"Wonderful, el Capitano," the Don sezs, "Bee-autiful! I am pleased muchos . . . an' now to the smartest crew I give the gift o' Don Alverez to the fine Yankee ship!"

Matey, we stiffened, each o' us bo's'ns bound to get the honor o' receivin' the port gift to our ship. Don Alverez walked along the deck, not quite hidin' the rollin' gait as told Davy he'd seen sea duty hisself, an' sudden-like, he stops before poor Bill Spunyarn who's bo's'n o' crew two.

"What can your crew do, amigo " Don asks civil.

"Nuthin', Sir, I'm bound to say, Sir," poor Bill sez.

"Surely somethin'," the Don sez kind, "Drill maybe?"

"No, Sir," Bill sez, sweatin', "we just can do as we're told an' no grumblin', Sir."

"Perhaps very excellent," Don Alverez sez an' on he walks to Tom Cringle's crew.

Now Tom salutes smart, his men standin' straight an' unwinkin', but not lookin' like they enjoyed it an' Tom sez, "Crew One, Sir. I taught 'em how to drill handsome, Sir."

An' Tom makes a smart about face an' bellers fitten to shiver the galley stove, " 'TTenshun! Right face; For'rard . . . march!" An' off goes Tom's crew, sour-faced but smart, paradin' around the decks with never a smile an' never a proud look for Tom. Tom sweats an' yells his orders an' once, when old Dick Morgan missed a step, he claps Dick smart with his ropes-end an' hisses annoyed, "This'll lose you a month's pay, you lubber"

The Don stands still. Davy sees he's impressed an' no blame to him. Finally, Tom ends his show, lookin' mighty pleased an' eyin' the gift an' the Don turns to your old shipmate Davy.

"Please, Sir," Davy sez, "I ain't never taught my boys no tricks; nary a one, sir, fitten to show off with."

"Well," the Don said, "what do you do best?"

Matey, Davy blushed, he did. What Davy's crew did best warn't to be compared to the fine show Tom Cringle had made. It warn't even as good as Bill Spunyarn's watch, who at least knew how to mind orders. "Well?" sez the Don.

"Boys," Davy sez, turnin' to his watch, "what do you like to do best? Well do it . . . an' handsome; the Don is a'waitin'!"

Davy'll never forgit that minute, me lad! Never! His crew shuffled an' stared at the deck an' finally one o' 'em starts to sing. Low an' sweet, it was, like only sailormen can sing an' it was the lovely shanty, Rio Bound. An' in a minute the others jined in an' the deep grand chorus filled the ship an' went echoin' 'gainst the dank cold stones of the fort on our beam.

The shanty finished, a'trailin' off like the last o' a sunset on the Line, an' Davy stands with his head hung. Tom Cringle had made the show; he'd won the governor's gift, sure.

"It ain't much," Davy said soft, "but, Sir, it's what my watch likes best. Tom's crew is worthy, Sir."

But the Don stood still, his eyes waverin' an' there wasn't a sound on the ship save the thin squeak o' a block aloft.

"Mister Shellback," Don Alverez sez, "I nigh forgot somethin' I learned at sea long ago. I'm obliged you reminded me, I am indeed. I like a crew as obeys orders. I like a crew as is smart an' perky. But what I like best is a crew as has not forgotten how to sing. A crew as sings is a happy crew an' a happy crew is one as has real leadership. Mister Shellback, when the gales is shriekin' an' I need real men aloft . . . 'twould be your crew I'd pick. You know why?"

"No, Sir," I sez.

"Because," the governor sez respeckful a'handin' me the

gift for the ship, "I wouldn't have to drive 'em. No ropes-end an' no orders . . . they'd follow their bo's'n a'singin' an' when they do that, by the Great Horn Spoon, the ship's got their brains an' the brawn an', what more, their HEARTS!"

An' that's a lesson, ain't it now, me Sea Scout bucko? Make your Crew love you; make 'em respeck you an' look up to you an' WANT to follow you. An' don't do it with a ropes-end or with bellerin' . . . just you be the finest man an' Scout you know how, just you be a friend an' a companion an' a shipmate, an' you, too, will have the hearts o' your crew. An' only with their hearts will your fine ship sail on an' on; only with their hearts will you yerself be a leader an' not a driver.

Fair weather, matey-lad . . . fair weather an' red skies always from your old friend and shipmate,

TWENTY THINGS FOR CREWS TO DO

I. CREW RADIO BROADCAST

Most local radio stations welcome the Boy Scouts of America in their studios and gladly arrange a series of broadcasts. Crews can very easily dramatize some of the fine scripts prepared by the National Office and obtainable through the Council Office without cost.

Here are some of special interest to Sea Scouts:

Scout Good Turn

Sea Scout Service

The Flood

Don't Give up the Ship

Two scripts of fine Eagle Scout stories are "Scout Adventures" and "Only an Eagle." "Storm Signals," and any of the dramatized Twelve Scout Laws make splendid presentations.

Unless the Ship boasts of experienced writing talent, it is seldom wise to write your own scripts. All broadcasting must be done only with the full permission and under the supervision of the Local Council — and then only after rehearsal under the studio director. Hints on broadcasting are obtainable from the Public Relations Service of the National Council, through the local Scout Executive.

2. CREW COLUMN IN THE SHIP'S PAPER

Many Sea Scout Ships publish Ship newspapers and each Crew ought to have a department in it. The Crew will select its own editor and reporter, turning the material over to the regular editor. Not only do local

179

Scouts and Scouters receive this paper but, by means of a National Sea Scout News Exchange, it is distributed throughout the country. Many of the articles appear later in such Scouting publications as the NATIONAL SEA SCOUT LOG, SCOUTING, LOCAL COUNCIL EXCHANGE and service pamphlets. Often the National office will request that Sea Scouts cover and report local Scouting events and it is a fine thing to see a credit line "Crew 3, S.S.S. Liberty" following a thrilling Scouting tale.

A Crew may even publish its own paper. If it does and wishes to join the Sea Scout News Exchange, arrangements must be made through the quartedeck with the Council Office. There are certain rules and standards (but no dues or fees) which must be adhered to and a regular application to fill out.

Some splendid Ship's papers which are full of ideas, are SEA SCOUT LUCKY BAG, Pony Express Council, St. Joseph, Mo.; RIDING LIGHT, S.S.S. Marblehead, Marblehead, Mass.; THE SPY GLASS, S.S.S. Golden Eagle, St. Louis, Mo.; THE BILGE PUMP, S.S.S. Flying Cloud, Omaha, Neb.; THE BARK, S.S.S. Sea Lion, Webster Groves, Mo. and the STAYSAIL, S.S.S. Sabine, New London, Conn. Perhaps sample copies might be obtained giving the Crew some ideas to work on.

3. CREW MERIT BADGE INSTRUCTORS

Any Crew can be of real service to Scouting by offering and being prepared to teach Troop Scouts of the Council the subject of Seamanship. The requirements for this Merit Badge are to be found in the Merit Badge Pamphlet, SEAMANSHIP. Not only will instruction from the pamphlet and THE SEA SCOUT MANUAL be helpful, but use of boats, life rings and other nautical gear will assure the candidate practical knowledge.

Such instruction can be done with a small group or individually but never at the Sea Scout meeting. It is a service entirely outside of Ship activities. Work closely with both the student's Scoutmaster and the Board of Review, using the same instruction methods as recommended in other parts of this handbook.

4. CREW MOVIES

The making of Sea Scout movies is a fascinating and instructive activity. After the story has been prepared (by someone who really can plot) a Sea Scout director plans the "shooting schedule" and "shots," and many meetings are held during which the actual movie is made. Great care must be exercised on timing, lighting, correct Sea Scout Uniform and ceremony and above all on continuity. The chief difficulty with amateur-made movies is the lack of story, or connection between scenes. Do not attempt a long story. For example, the Sea Scout Bridge of Honor would discover the hero dressing at home, arguing his father into borrowing the car, his dog looking wistfully at him as he leaves (to be petted, of course), the car speeding to the "gal's" house; then a cut to the girl, powdering. The Sea Scout rings the doorbell, the girl isn't ready but her father hauls out a ship model and talks about it to the Sea Scout. They become engrossed and the girl stands in the hall tapping her foot. Finally, the Sea Scout "comes to," he feels badly about his carelessness, apologizes, all is rosy, — or isn't it? — they leave — etc., etc. The important thing is that there is a head man, a hero; to whom you have given character, problems, conflict and a stake. How he works them out is the suspense of the story. Worked out against the background of a Bridge of Honor it not only depicts a Bridge of Honor but it shows how Sea Scout training in courtesy, and gentlemanliness (remember the Sea Scout apologized!) reflects itself.

Rehearse every scene until it's right. Use make-up for night and indoor shots. Get simple backgrounds without MOTION, unless the script demands it. Have your Local Council check it for policy. Cut it and edit it carefully. If you need sub-titles, borrow a black velvet "letter-board" such as the lunch wagon uses for its daily menu. Letter out the title and shoot it with a portrait lens under shadowless light.

The manufacturers of movie machines and projectors issue many helpful hints for your guidance.

5. CREW EMERGENCY SIGNAL STATION

There is a blizzard; wires are down. A fire breaks out. The siren won't work — but the fire-chief fought through the snow to a Crew Leader's home. All he said was, "call out the gang." In minutes the Sea Scout Crew were knocking at doors, routing out the members of the volunteer fire department..

An hour later a telegraph operator knocked. He had nine important messages that he couldn't phone. The Sea Scouts delivered them. This is an actual case.

Both the fire-chief and the telegraph operator knew, because it had been pre-arranged, where to go for help. This Crew had long ago set up the organization for an emergency signal station. They were faithful to the motto Be Prepared.

6. CREW WATERFRONT BEAUTIFICATION PROJECT

Very few waterfronts there are that could not stand some cleaning up and improving. Here are some of the things a Crew might do.

Supply waste paper barrels, painted and serviced.

20 THINGS FOR

Plant trees, shrubbery and grass.

Remove wrecks, derelicts and low-tide unsightliness.

Provide dinghy floats, stakes or mooring rings.

Provide warning signs or rails on dangerous wharves, walls, etc.

Dig out stagnant pools so that the tide or current cleans them.

Arrange a flagpole and the flying of the American Flag daily.

In all cases it must be remembered that the crew must work only with the permission of the park department, town boards or private owners concerned. Council advice is a good thing to have before planning civic undertakings of any kind.

7. THE STORM PATROL

"The home port of the S.S.S. Dauntless is Noank, Connecticut. It is subject, during certain times of the year, to terrific lashings by gales and giant seas from the storm quarters. Much damage has been the usual toll of these "snorters" but thanks to the Storm Patrol, formed by the three crews of twenty-two men and officers of the Ship, such damage recently has been kept to a minimum. Upon the forecasting of a storm, either by radio, the newspapers or the weather bureau station nearby, each Crew at once proceeds to its assigned patrol area. Small boats are hauled to a safe inshore point, lobstermen and draggers are warned and assisted to take their vessels to safety up the river; pots, pot buoys and gear are secured and removed from the reach of the surf. All persons, particularly children, are warned from docks and piers. The crews are divided into watches which keep constant guard during the storm, always with an eye to sea for vessels which have been caught out. Very important is the "Town

Detail" which searches for sagging electric wires, split trees and limbs and loose shutters, signboards, etc. All units are ready to communicate with Coast Guard, State Police and highway authorities.

"So far property valued at well over $2,000 has been actually saved by Sea Scouts. It is a real service, appreciated by the citizens of the town, cheerfully, and, of course, freely given. Sea Scouts eye every dark cloud or sudden wind and storm gear is often in evidence hours before a storm breaks." (HANDBOOK FOR SKIPPERS.)

Then, in 1938 an impossible thing happened in New England. A savage West Indian hurricane went on the rampage; came growling and devouring at Noank.

Every Sea Scout, in every Crew of the S.S.S. Dauntless was ready for it! The story of the Dauntless and its hurricane service—of the brave and humane deeds of its Crews, during and for days after the disaster, has become one of the sagas of Scouting.

Read that story to your Crew. It's in Chapter XVII of the HANDBOOK FOR SKIPPERS; it has appeared in American and English Scouting literature, it is the subject of a Scout Radio Script (No. 3909) was the subject of a sermon, and is reprinted in a Take-Me-Home pamphlet!

The "preparedness" of the Motto "Be Prepared" was behind the wonderful Scout rescue stories of the Ohio flood, the Florida hurricane, the earthquakes of California and Montana, the twisters of Murphysboro and Gainsville.

Any Crew can organize into a Storm Patrol. It is hoped that its services will never be needed—which should be the very last reason in the world to regard it as anything but a live, important organization.

Then, too, a Storm Patrol is excellent training for participation in an Emergency Service Corps.

8. EMERGENCY SERVICE CORPS

It was late afternoon. The storm signals had been set since early morning. The Coast Guard had been on duty for twenty-four hours straight. A gale was lashing the coast line. Trees had fallen making the coastal roads almost impassable.

Bo's'n Jones of the S.S.S. Flying Cloud sat hovering over his short-wave radio outfit in the basement of his home one mile from Indian Head Rock. He was following the signals from the Coast Guard up and down the coast. Until 4 o'clock no ship had been in danger. Bo's'n Jones knew that his fellow Crew members would soon be gathering in their basement rendezvous, since it was Crew meeting night. His Assistant, Bo's'n's Mate Murphy, was the first to arrive. As they sat talking, the persistent noise of the short wave radio interrupted their conversation.

"S. O. S. . . . S. O. S. . . ."

They stopped. They listened. The call was from the "Vandalia" The gale had battered her. She was floundering off Indian Head Rock. They listened.

Finally word came through from the Coast Guard that they were four hours away from the "Vandalia." Bo's'n Jones tapped a message out to the Coast Guard.

"We can reach the Vandalia with a breeches buoy. Should we go ahead? Emergency Service Crew, S.S.S. Flying Cloud, Bo's'n Jones."

Word flashed from the Commandant of the Coast Guard: "Try. Best of luck. Commandant P. J. Smith."

By that time three more members had gathered with Bo's'n Jones and Bo's'n's Mate Murphy. Things were happening. Tackle was being brought out. Sou'westers were being taken out of the sea chest. Jim Larkin had been sent to round up the other members of the Crew. Their equipment was loaded into a truck and hurried to the beach. In less time than it takes to tell the Sea

CREWS TO DO 185

Scouts set up the equipment, shot a line to the "Vandalia" and set the breeches buoy operating. In this way more than forty passengers aboard the ship were saved.

Sea Scouts all over America are ready at a minute's notice to answer any emergency call. You have read the story of the "Dauntless." There was a ship in which every member was ready when the moment for action came.

Be prepared and then Do — the Sea Scout motto! By planning in advance what your Crew would do should storm, or flood, or fire come to your neighborhood brings life to this motto.

Under quarterdeck guidance your Crew can set up the machinery for an Emergency Service Patrol, and under its Crew Leader can practice frequently. Your Emergency Service Patrol, of course, is a unit of the Council or District Emergency Service Corps. It must be clearly understood that the Emergency Service Patrol carries on its activities in cooperation with the Council or District Emergency Service Corps, and that the Emergency Service Corps is subordinate to authority by their community, county or state police departments, American Red Cross local chapter or national staff.

Emergency Service Corps in no way compete with or duplicate the work of the American Red Cross, but merely supplement it. Sea Scouts must, of course, take no responsibilities which should be carried on by adults. Remember, DISASTER RELIEF WORK IS IN THE MAIN, OF COURSE, THE TASK OF ADULTS.

The program of the Emergency Service Corps is set up to do two things:

(1) To prepare for Emergency Service when conditions are normal.

(2) To effectively carry on the relief program when the Emergency arrives.

While Sea Scouts in the case of extreme emergency will be ready to do almost any sort of work, definite restrictions are set up to be operative in all but the most unusual circumstances. Here are certain things that are proper and possible for Sea Scout activities as well as a list of different activities to be done only when other help is not available.

First Group — (Limited to members of the Emergency Service Corps)

Communications, which may include foot, bicycle, boat, radio signals, carrier pigeons, motorcycle or car.

Photography.

First Aid, including transportation when necessary.

Rescue Work *when under expert direction.*

Construction and supervision of sanitary equipment.

Erection of tents and other shelters.

Providing entertainment to refugees.

Second Group — TO BE DONE ONLY UNDER EXTRAORDINARY CIRCUMSTANCES (Limited to members of the Emergency Service Corps)

Direction of traffic.

Policing of sanitary equipment, sleeping quarters or washing facilities.

Handling of soiled clothing for distribution.

Burying of animals, etc.

Sea Scouts should not be expected to do work in refugee camps which might properly be expected to be the legitimate task of the refugees themselves or, which would provide legitimate labor for needy workers if not done by Scouts. Such questionable activities including cooking and serving, kitchen police duties including dish washing, policing of latrines or quarters, and handling clothing, bedding, etc. This is not intended to imply that Sea Scouts would refuse to do these things if conditions make it necessary, but, rather, that they should not continue it beyond a reasonable period.

CREWS TO DO   187

Third Group — Those things which can be done by Scouts under fifteen years of age under leadership of members of the Emergency Service Corps, under conditions which will offer a maximum of protection for the younger boys involved:

Orderlies and messengers; assisting in the registration of refugees; distributing food, when necessary; collecting, sorting, and distributing clothing (under sanitary conditions only); preparing tags and identification cards for refugees; distributing notices, handbills and generally stimulating citizens to meet financial needs for the purpose of aiding those in distress, BUT IN NO INSTANCE HANDLING CASH.

The uniform for Sea Scouts in all emergency relief work is the official Sea Scout Uniform, supplemented with rain coats, sou'westers, *dungarees,* all bearing in large letters the designation "Emergency Service Corps, Boy Scouts of America." Every member of the Corps should be encouraged to have on hand, ready for use, wool underwear and socks, and ear protectors and mittens in sections subject to intense cold. Any supplemental equipment should also bear the distinguishing letters: "Emergency Service Corps, Boy Scouts of America."

Every qualified member of the Emergency Service Corps wears its emblem on his Sea Scout blouse. When on active duty, an arm brassard is also worn. Every qualified member should carry in his pocket his Emergency Service Corps identification card, bearing his photograph and finger-print.

Emergency Service Apprentice — The Emergency Service Apprentice Rating Plan is for First Class Scouts of proved physical fitness who declare their determination to join the Emergency Service Corps and take the required training for promotion into the corps as soon as possible.

20 THINGS FOR

9. EMERGENCY SERVICE TRAINING PLAN

Today, with our Scout Program of Action for Strengthening and Invigorating Democracy, it becomes the duty of the Sea Scout Crew to prepare itself ever better for community service. Every Sea Scout Requirement has added significance and every Rank or Merit Badge obtained will indicate additional preparation.

Under the Emergency Service Training Plan (see the pamphlet "Emergency Service Training Plan"), the Sea Scout Crews and Ships plan and accent that part of the Sea Scout Program which will best afford training in the following classifications:

1. Physical fitness. Health and physical development.
2. Observation, identification and memory.
   Knowledge of directions, navigational conditions, shore marks, both natural and man-made, in the home waters, a familiarity with the compass so that orientation may be accurately accomplished.
3. Communication.
   By all methods of signaling both night and day, by rowboats, canoes and launches, by land travel and running, by swimming.
4. Outdoor Living.
   By greater emphasis of actually living on ship board, Sea Scout bases or shore camps, especial emphasis upon off-the-country living, by the preparation of food. Every Sea Scout should have at his finger tips several filling recipes and methods of preparation under emergency conditions both ashore and afloat. Sleeping, including use of blankets and ground cloths. Preparation of fire woods with axe and saw. Fire prevention and suppression.
5. Safety.
   Safety will be a part of everything taught.
   Safety with firearms, signal flares and rockets.

CREWS TO DO   189

The use of the belt hatchet and three-fourths size axe, and the care and sharpening and safe use of these tools.

Fire prevention and suppression on ship board and water-side places.

The making of fire suppression equipment.

6. Preservations of Human Life.

Water rescue skills with boats, rescue equipment and by swimming. First aid for arterial bleeding, suffocation, poison, exposure and burns. Comprehensive instruction on transportation of injured persons.

7. Food Supply, Production and Conservation.

Fish and shell-fish hatching.

The quantity catching of fish such as netting, seining, and trapping.

The raising of small birds and animals for food.

To these seven training emphases, may be added many others. They should be of a type fitted to the need and will probably be selected by the District or Council Leaders in charge of Emergency Service Training.

As important as any part of the training is for the Crew to act and think as an integral part of the Ship and for the individual Sea Scout to adjust himself to the task of serving his Crew. There are many activities in the Sea Scout Program which, without any charge whatsoever, will instruct both the Crew and the individual in the spirit of this training plan. It is merely a question of properly selecting the activities and accents best suited to your own particular community.

In the course of time and with little expense, Crews can be equipped or equip themselves with a number of valuable pieces of emergency gear. It can make and keep on hand efficient stretchers, various types of bandages, fire fighting equipment, properly equipped boats, signal apparatus and water rescue equipment. A basis of such a collection might well commence with the gathering of inexpensive familiar objects such as axes, shovels, rope, blankets, kerosene lanterns, signal flags, ring buoys, etc. Naturally, these should be frequently inspected and kept always ready for instant service.

The decision of the Crew to engage in an Emergency Service Training Plan is a fine and noble one. It should be remembered, however, that such a group, unless closely allied with the District or Council training plan is of very little real value. A very fine thing for a Sea Scout Crew to do — and this is simple because the Sea Scout is an older fellow and because his program has already given him preliminary training — is to perfect itself in some phase of emergency work closely connected with the water and offer itself as a demonstration squad and instructing group to Scout Troops in the Council.

10. TRAINING FOR MOBILIZATION

Over the years experience in mobilization of Scouts and Scouters on short notice and in an efficient manner has enabled the Boy Scouts of America to render services of inestimable value. (See the pamphlet "Training for Mobilization.") The way to insure efficiency in mobilization is to develop, with the aid of Ship and Council Officers, a mobilization system and to practice it frequently under conditions that give the Crew something satisfying to do. When they are mobilized for this practice, the purposes may be quite simple: perhaps merely for rowing practice, a community service or the attendance at a football game. The important thing about it is the actual speed and efficiency of the mobilization plans.

Pre-mobilization plans should see to the following important items:

1. Parents should be thoroughly acquainted with the purpose of the mobilization and their permission solic-

ited for their sons to participate.

2. Set up and agree on a code word to designate the mobilization, perhaps the expression "All-Hands" would be one. This would save endless explaining. Work out ways of rousing sleeping boys and quickly getting the mobilization call to them.

3. Arrange a fool-proof method of contacting each member of the Crew, Telephones, bicycles, autos and boats are often useless during an emergency. Use the above methods if possible, but put your real faith on the Sea Scout's running or walking.

4. Make arrangements with school authorities and employers so that a call may be issued at any time of the day.

5. A definite place should be designated in advance for all mobilizations.

6. A definite course of action should be put into immediate effect so that as the Crew members arrive at the mobilization point, full instructions will be awaiting them.

Training for mobilization should be geared in with the plans of the District or Council Emergency Service Corps Officers. As a badge of recognition the Sea Scout Uniform should be worn. The Sea Scout should bear in mind that failure to perform the duties assigned to him might result in disaster for the entire project.

11. CREW CHRISTMAS PROJECT

Nothing makes for Crew spirit more than the adventure of sharing a good deed. At Christmas time, Thanksgiving or Easter, when our happiness can never be fully complete because of those others who are less fortunate than we — the Crew can find a real reason for its existence by doing a Good Turn. These may include:

Christmas baskets for the needy.

Reconditioning toys for children.

A play or demonstration for crippled children or orphans.

Helping old people shop in the crowded stores.

Supplying transportation for the aged to and from church services.

Supplying and decorating an outdoor tree in a low-income section of the town.

Anything that is unselfish and good and helpful to others without thought of personal gain or publicity, is indicated. Sometimes it takes a great deal of tact to do a Good Turn and your Sea Scout Leaders should be consulted about your plans.

12. CREW PLAYS

There are many occasions such as Father and Son dinners, or Open Ship Nights or District meetings when a short Scout play fits into the program. No group is better equipped to stage this than the Crew. Your dramatics teacher or English instructor at school will have scores of simple one-act plays that your Crew could present.

Remember to select a simple one, without too much scenery or too many props required and rehearse it well. Any kind of presentation is better for a little "staging" and due attention should be given to lighting, timing, and the illusion of reality. If you can get the services of a coach, so much the better. Remember, that your Crew appears as a part of the Boy Scouts of America. They must wear the correct uniform and do only things that Scouts can and would do, if the subject is one of Scouting.

The Merit Badge pamphlet on DRAMATICS will prove a boon to the histrionically inclined Crew.

CREWS TO DO 193

13. SEA SCOUT BOAT LAUNCHING PARTY

The occasion of the annual launching of the Ship's boat or boats provides an opportunity for a fine party.

The launching ceremony is carried out with all the pomp and realism of a large vessel. Young ladies are invited and evening entertainment or dancing provided.

Don't forget a "work" detail, Sea Scouts in dungarees to care for the boat after she has been launched. She should be re-christened, of course. Music adds to the affair.

Here is the Launching Ceremony used by the S.S.S. Dauntless upon the refitting and commissioning of a 26-foot Monomoy Surf Boat, procured from the Coast Guard through National Headquarters.

5:00 Assembly at shore base. Mixed party. Uniformed, of course.

5:15 Address by Lieut. ———, U.S.C.G. A History of the Monomoy Boats.

5:25 Prayer by local pastor.

5:28 Christening (by young lady elected by Ship).

5:30 Launching (to bugle, cheers, etc.).

5:35 Good wishes for smooth sailing (Council Commodore).

5:40 Tiller presented to Skipper (Commissioning).

5:45 Lobster roast at Base.

7:00 Evening sail in small boats (all hands).

8:30 Dance (Sea Scout Hall).

11:00 Taps.

14. A CREW LAND CRUISE

Cruises are usually considered as being taken upon the water or by attending Scout Camp and engaging in a lively water program. Land cruises can also be made and it provides a lusty activity at times when the boats are de-commissioned or the weather bad for sailing.

20 THINGS FOR

They may be made by a hike, or in a car (preferably one Crew in a station wagon or light truck, or in a public conveyance).

To some extent, a regular cruise program is followed, a log kept, watches stood and Sea Scout custom and tradition adhered to. Some fine land cruises have been as follows:

To a distant Marine Museum — by truck.

To a Coast Defense Fort — by private car, transferring to Sound steamer and beach hike.

To the Regional Flagship — by public bus.

To a Regional Regatta — train and formation hike through visited city (Boston).

To a Navy Yard, as guests on board the Frigate "Constitution" — by station wagon.

To an island lighthouse — by car and lighthouse tender.

To the start of a yacht race — truck and riverside hike.

To college shell races — hired party boat and car.

Scout Camp week-end cruise (cabin) — bikes.

15. CREW TABLEAUX

Once a year, during Boy Scout Week in February, students in most American schools are permitted and encouraged to appear for classes in Scout or Sea Scout Uniforms. This is a fine reminder to America that Scouting is backing up the work of the educator.

In many schools, the authorities will cooperate to the extent of allowing a few extra moments at morning assembly for special recognition of the week. These exercises may include a speaker or a Scout movie. Any Sea Scout Crew can add color to it by offering to present a closing tableau.

Subjects for these tableaus are many. One of the finest sources is the annual calendar which the artist,

Mr. Norman Rockwell, a Scout himself, paints. These scenes live and are tremendously human and striking. To present, with soft music, proper and dramatic lighting, the current calendar picture is a fine Crew activity. "Scout Family" is another tableau which stirs; so is the "March of the Pioneers" or the "Landing of the Pilgrims." The imaginative Crew Leader, working with the quarterdeck and the school authorities, can think of many more subjects.

16. APPRENTICE TO A. B. IN 60 MINUTES

Dads like Sea Scouting! But they are lubbers, Bo's'n!

Capitalize on the fun in this situation by holding a Crew Dad Advancement Night. Here's a suggested program:

Dads are formed into a group, several Crew Leaders are assigned as instructors and advisors. They are taught the Scout Salute, the Scout Oath and then make application to join the Crew.

Apprentice Tests are immediately given as follows (all burlesqued):

1. Bend from the hips ten times — then test wind (Med. Exam.).

2. Make a noise like a foghorn (or a bell).

3. Give the Scout Salute.

Immediately create them Apprentices. Then:

1. Show how to row a boat, sitting on a chair.

2. Show how to rescue a spent swimmer (two Dads on floor).

3. Make a model boat by chewing a stick of gum and modeling the cud with a toothpick.

Immediately create them Ordinary Seamen. Then:

1. Act out being a sloop in a fair wind. A catboat (crying, "Me-ow") in a strong gale. A side-wheel paddle steamer.

2. Show (jumping from chairs) two diving positions.

3. Knot-tying contest (three simple knots).

MOCK BRIDGE OF HONOR

1. Dads must dance with each other.

2. Give them Able Bodied Insignia (a large cardboard anchor tied to neck).

3. End up with a feed, chowder or refreshments — chantey-singing, Sea Scout Movie.

The idea is FUN — not only for the Crew, but for the Dads!

17. CREW SCRAP (OR LOG) BOOK

The contents of the scrapbook may take the range from photos and dance-orders to examination papers and comic drawings. Most Crews can take care of this splendidly.

The exterior of the scrapbook, however, can be made unique and outstanding by applying a little Crew thought. Scrapbooks can take the form of water-casks, drums, model boats which open, or be in book form bound with brass or wood or tooled leather. Some Crew scrapbooks have been made in the form of miniature sea chests, others bound with sennit work in the style of the old Royal Navy.

18. MONEY-MAKING IDEAS FOR THE CREW

Every Ship that has a real program of DO and MAKE, needs money. Ways and means are discussed and voted upon by the Ship; Skipper approval gained; and the Crew turns to. There are literally hundreds of ways to make money. Remember always: Crew money-making activities should never take work away from anyone who needs it. They should not violate in spirit or fact Child Labor Laws, nor the commercial policy of the Boy Scouts of America.

CREWS TO DO 197

Pay for labor should not be of the "price-cutting" variety. A good job for a good price. The sincere and ambitious crew is MAN labor; regardless of who pushes a lawn-mower, if the lawn is mowed well and neatly the job is worth standard prices usually paid for this type of work.

Make handicraft articles (Chapter 10, HANDBOOK FOR PATROL LEADERS).

Sell magazine subscriptions (see the BOYS' LIFE Agent Plan).

Make and sell ship weather-vanes.

Plant trees and shrubbery.

Develop and print snapshots.

Take care of furnace, lawns, ashes, screens.

Take care of pets during owner's absence.

Care for a yacht.

Dig and sell bait, clams or oysters.

Sell greeting cards.

Repair ship models.

Raise tropical fish.

Collect and sell old junk, paper, etc.

Conduct a hobby exchange.

Repair docks and landings for private owners.

Maintain an island ferry service.

Teach summer visitors sailing, swimming and diving.

Collect and sell sea shells and sponges to curio shops.

Burn iron from wrecks and sell.

All the money is turned over to the Ship Purser and the Yeoman keeps record of it. It is spent only after agreement by the Ship.

19. CREW MEMORIAL EXERCISES

Within the Crew meeting, it is often fitting and Scouting, to observe with brief exercises or mere mention, great naval events, disasters of the sea or the anniversary of a new era in man's conquest of the great

20 THINGS FOR

oceans of the globe. This dramatizes sea history.

Columbus Day to the Sea Scout means not only the discovery of America but the successful completion of a famous and daring voyage. The Crew observe Columbus Day from this angle.

The sinking of the Titanic, as well as the establishment of the International Ice Patrol, is an event which the Sea Scout Crew might observe each April 14th. Discussion of the tragedy by the Crew Leader might be held, the story of the Titanic disaster might be read from LUBBERS AFLOAT (reading time: 15 minutes) or a Crew presentation be given of the actual ceremony as held annually over the grave of the Titanic.

The following material was prepared by Chief Bo's'n's Mate, L. O. Pressey of the U. S. Coast Guard and an active Scout Commissioner of Pequot Council, New London, Conn.

CEREMONIES OF THE SEA IN SEA SCOUTING

A Scout is Reverent. We, as Sea Scouts, still carry on the laws of the Scout and for that reason many of our ceremonies are very good examples of the Twelfth Scout Law.

Anyone who has ever heard of the U. S. Coast Guard knows that it is this service that carries out the International Ice Patrol. This patrol is maintained for the purpose of preventing another disaster like the sinking of the Titanic, in which so many lives were lost. The International Ice Patrol is maintained by the U. S. Coast Guard and the expense is divided among the maritime nations and in that way the shipping of the world is protected from icebergs. Any vessel navigating the North Atlantic will at some time cross the path of the icebergs as they float down from the ice cap. The Ice Patrol watches for each berg and reports its condition

CREWS TO DO   199

and position each day to the ships at sea. This information is given daily until the berg reaches the Gulf Stream where the warm water quickly melts the ice and it is no longer a menace to navigation. One man known as the oceanographer is transferred each time a vessel is relieved and for that reason never leaves the ice lanes until icebergs cease to appear. So, if the patrol lasts for three or four months, he is never in sight of land, and about the only thing he will see is ice and the different crews on each ship. We may say, "What a lonely life!" It is, in a way, but this man is doing a very worthwhile job when we realize that not a life has been lost on account of bergs since patrols of the ice lanes were started and the data collected by the oceanographer are the means by which predictions are made each year when the bergs will start appearing.

The foregoing is a brief outline of the International Ice Patrol. Knowing the fondness of most Sea Scouts for ceremonies and how they fit into the program, it seems something should be told of the rites of the sea as used in commemoration of a sea tragedy of the twentieth century. A very solemn and reverent service is held on each anniversary of the Titanic's sinking. The patrol vessel having the duty at that time makes a point of reaching the position 41:46 N Latitude and 50:14 W Longitude at noon April 14; General muster of the crew is held, with all hands in dress blues. The enlisted men are mustered aft on the port side, all commissioned officers are mustered on the starboard side. The firing squad is forward of the officers and the church pennant is hoisted above the National Colors on the flagstaff. A prayer is offered for the lives lost in the disaster, after which the entire crew and officers remove their hats. A passage is read from the Bible and then three volleys are fired over the spot where 1,517 lives were lost. A wreath is then dropped over the side and this is the end of a traditional salute to the lives lost in the worst iceberg disaster of all time. The church pennant is then lowered and the National Colors hoisted to full mast and the usual routine of the Ice Patrol is carried on.

20. CREW CHURCH ATTENDANCE

The Crew which is living the Scout way, makes the Twelfth Scout Law a vital part of its life. The Crew, when it attends Church as a group, wears the uniform, and meticulously observes the standards of a gentleman and a Scout. If the Church has reserved a certain section for the Crew, it files to its place in quiet order. Hats are uniformly held, and the Crew carefully adheres to the ritual and observances of the Church. Crew members thank the minister as they leave.

Crew Leaders are cautioned that each man of the Crew has the right and responsibility to exercise his own religious preferences and is never to be forced to attend the religious services of any other sect.

PARTS FOR A LAND SHIP.

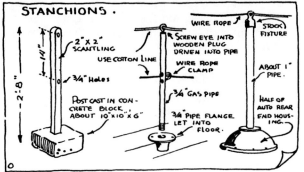

STANCHIONS.

WIRE ROPE

STOCK FIXTURE

2" X 2" SCANTLING

14"

2'-8"

SCREW EYE INTO WOODEN PLUG DRIVEN INTO PIPE

USE COTTON LINE

WIRE ROPE CLAMP

¾" Holes

ABOUT 1" PIPE.

¾" GAS PIPE

POST CAST IN CONCRETE BLOCK, ABOUT 10"X10"X 6"

¾" PIPE FLANGE LET INTO FLOOR.

HALF OF AUTO REAR END HOUSING.

O

GANGWAYS.

MAKE 2   PORT & STARBOARD

ARC PIECES OF 2" FIR OR PINE . PLANK WITH 1" X 3" FIR. PAINT BATTLESHIP GRAY.

RUBBER MATTING

3"

ABOUT 4 FEET

28"

HAULING LINES

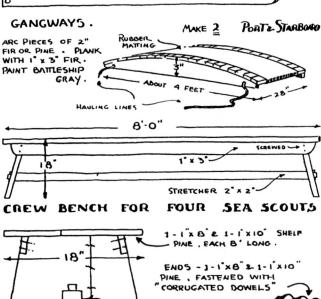

8'-0"

SCREWED →

18"

1" X 3"

STRETCHER 2" X 2"

CREW BENCH FOR FOUR SEA SCOUTS

18"

1 - 1"X 8" & 1 - 1"X10" SHELF PINE , EACH 8' LONG.

ENDS - 1 - 1"X 8" & 1 - 1"X10" PINE , FASTENED WITH "CORRUGATED DOWELS"

STRETCHER MORTISED AND PINNED.

C D L

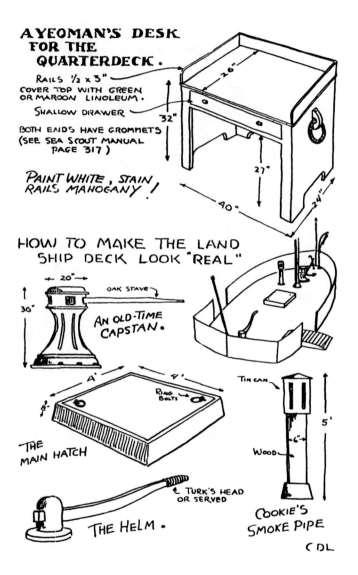

A YEOMAN'S DESK FOR THE QUARTERDECK.

RAILS ½ x 3"
COVER TOP WITH GREEN OR MAROON LINOLEUM.

SHALLOW DRAWER

BOTH ENDS HAVE GROMMETS (SEE SEA SCOUT MANUAL PAGE 317)

PAINT WHITE, STAIN RAILS MAHOGANY!

26"

32"

27"

40"

24"

HOW TO MAKE THE LAND SHIP DECK LOOK "REAL"

20"

36"

OAK STAVE

AN OLD-TIME CAPSTAN.

4'

4'

8"

RING BOLTS

THE MAIN HATCH

TIN CAN

WOOD

6"

5'

COOKIE'S SMOKE PIPE

TURK'S HEAD OR SERVED

THE HELM.

CDL

CREWS TO MAKE

A FIFE RAIL
FOR THE LAND SHIP.

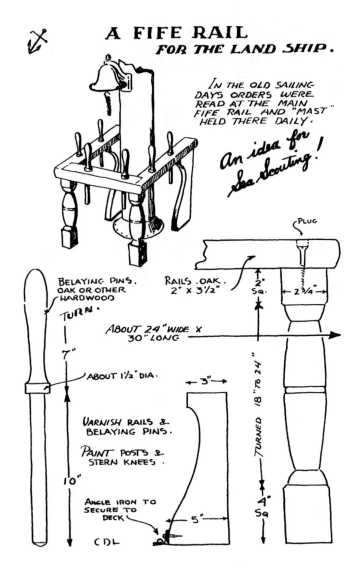

In the old sailing-days orders were read at the main fife rail and "mast" held there daily.

An idea for Sea Scouting !

Belaying pins. Oak or other hardwood

TURN.

7"

ABOUT 1½" DIA.

Varnish rails & belaying pins.

Paint posts & stern knees.

10"

Angle iron to secure to deck

CDL

Rails . Oak . 2" × 3½"

About 24" wide × 30" long

3"

5"

PLUG

2" Sq.

2¾"

TURNED 18" to 24"

4" Sq.

A SALUTING CANNON.

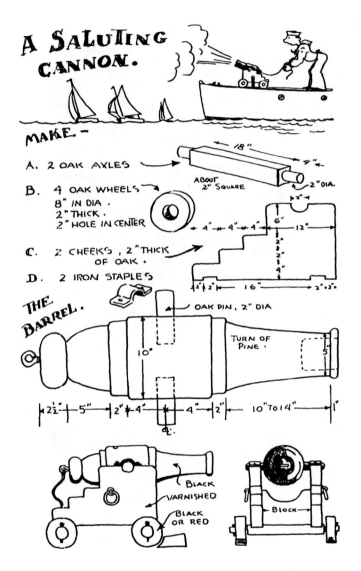

MAKE -

A. 2 OAK AXLES

18" · 4"
ABOUT 2" SQUARE
2" DIA.

B. 4 OAK WHEELS
8" IN DIA.
2" THICK.
2" HOLE IN CENTER

4" · 4" · 4" · 6" · 12"
2"
2"
2"
4"

C. 2 CHEEKS, 2" THICK
OF OAK.

2" · 2" · 16" · 2" · 2"

D. 2 IRON STAPLES

THE BARREL.

OAK PIN, 2" DIA

10"

TURN OF PINE.

5"

2½" · 5" · 2" · 4" · 4" · 2" · 10" TO 14" · 1"

♀.

BLACK VARNISHED

BLACK OR RED

BLOCK

CREWS TO MAKE

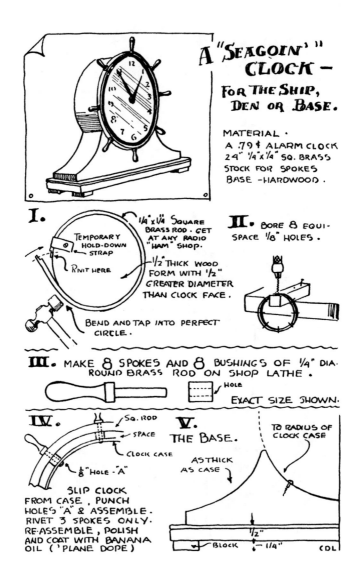

A "SEAGOIN'" CLOCK —

FOR THE SHIP, DEN OR BASE.

MATERIAL ·
A .79¢ ALARM CLOCK
24" ¼"x¼" SQ. BRASS
STOCK FOR SPOKES
BASE -HARDWOOD.

I. ¼"x¼" SQUARE BRASS ROD. GET AT ANY RADIO "HAM" SHOP.

TEMPORARY HOLD-DOWN STRAP

RIVIT HERE

½" THICK WOOD FORM WITH ½" GREATER DIAMETER THAN CLOCK FACE.

BEND AND TAP INTO PERFECT CIRCLE.

II. BORE 8 EQUI-SPACE ⅛" HOLES.

III. MAKE 8 SPOKES AND 8 BUSHINGS OF ¼" DIA. ROUND BRASS ROD ON SHOP LATHE.

HOLE

EXACT SIZE SHOWN.

IV. SQ. ROD

SPACE

CLOCK CASE

⅛" HOLE - "A"

SLIP CLOCK FROM CASE, PUNCH HOLES "A" & ASSEMBLE. RIVET 3 SPOKES ONLY. RE-ASSEMBLE, POLISH AND COAT WITH BANANA OIL ('PLANE DOPE)

V. THE BASE.

TO RADIUS OF CLOCK CASE

AS THICK AS CASE

½"

BLOCK

¼"

CDL

MODEL BUOYS.

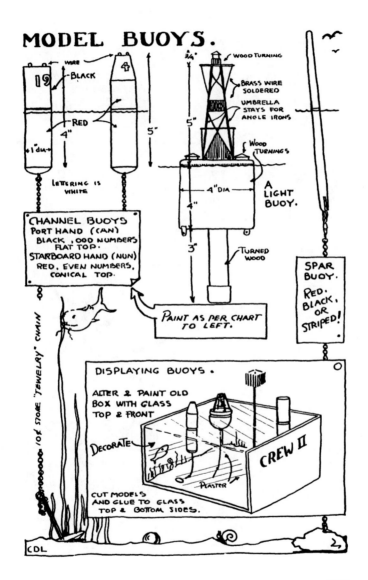

WIRE

BLACK

19

4

WOOD TURNING

BRASS WIRE
SOLDERED

UMBRELLA
STAYS FOR
ANGLE IRONS

RED

4"

5"

3/4"

5'

WOOD
TURNINGS

+ 1"dia+

LETTERING IS
WHITE

A
LIGHT
BUOY.

4" DIA

4"

CHANNEL BUOYS
PORT HAND (CAN)
BLACK , ODD NUMBERS
FLAT TOP.
STARBOARD HAND (NUN)
RED, EVEN NUMBERS,
CONICAL TOP.

3"

TURNED
WOOD

10' OF STORE "JEWELRY" CHAIN

PAINT AS PER CHART
TO LEFT.

SPAR
BUOY.

RED,
BLACK,
OR
STRIPED!

DISPLAYING BUOYS.

ALTER & PAINT OLD
BOX WITH GLASS
TOP & FRONT

DECORATE

PLASTER

CREW II

CUT MODELS
AND GLUE TO GLASS
TOP & BOTTOM SIDES.

CDL

CREWS TO MAKE

FANCY LOGS.

EVERY SHIP STRIVING FOR "FLAGSHIP" RATING MUST SUBMIT A FANCY LOG.

Some Ideas!

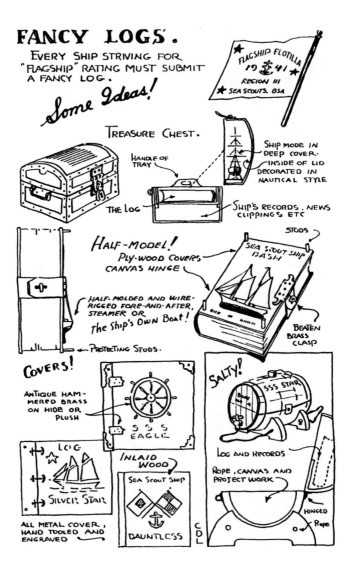

FLAGSHIP FLOTILLA
19 41
REGION III
SEA SCOUTS, BSA

TREASURE CHEST.

HANDLE OF TRAY

THE LOG

SHIP MADE IN DEEP COVER. INSIDE OF LID DECORATED IN NAUTICAL STYLE

SHIP'S RECORDS, NEWS CLIPPINGS ETC

STUDS

HALF-MODEL!
PLY-WOOD COVERS
CANVAS HINGE

SEA SCOUT SHIP DASH

HALF-MOLDED AND WIRE-RIGGED FORE-AND-AFTER, STEAMER OR *the Ship's Own Boat!*

PROTECTING STUDS.

BEATEN BRASS CLASP

COVERS!

ANTIQUE HAMMERED BRASS ON HIDE OR PLUSH

S S S EAGLE

SALTY!

SSS STAR

LOG AND RECORDS

ROPE, CANVAS AND PROJECT WORK

HINGED

Rope

LOG
SILVER STAR

INLAID WOOD

SEA SCOUT SHIP

DAUNTLESS

ALL METAL COVER, HAND TOOLED AND ENGRAVED

20 THINGS FOR

SWAB THE DECK.

A NOVEL SEA SCOUT ADVANCEMENT CHART.

KEEP YOUR DECK CLEAN —

ADVANCE!

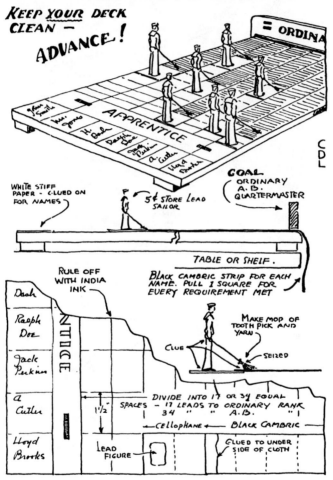

= ORDINA

GOAL
ORDINARY
A. B.
QUARTERMASTER

WHITE STIFF PAPER - GLUED ON FOR NAMES

5¢ STORE LEAD SAILOR

TABLE OR SHELF.

RULE OFF WITH INDIA INK

BLACK CAMBRIC STRIP FOR EACH NAME. PULL 1 SQUARE FOR EVERY REQUIREMENT MET

MAKE MOP OF TOOTH PICK AND YARN

GLUE

SEIZED

DIVIDE INTO 17 OR 34 EQUAL SPACES - 17 LEADS TO ORDINARY RANK 34 " " A.B. " 1

CELLOPHANE ← BLACK CAMBRIC

LEAD FIGURE

GLUED TO UNDER SIDE OF CLOTH

CREWS TO MAKE

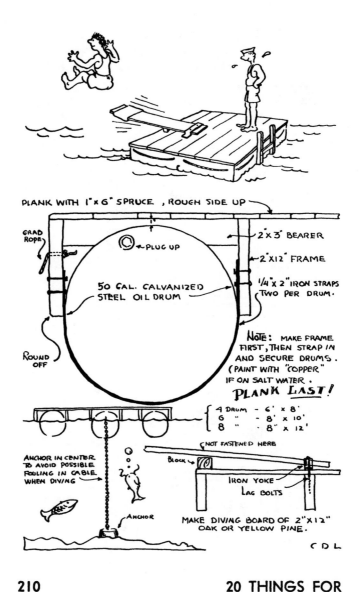

PLANK WITH 1"x 6" SPRUCE , ROUGH SIDE UP

GRAB ROPE

←PLUG UP

2"x 3" BEARER

2"x 12" FRAME

50 GAL. GALVANIZED STEEL OIL DRUM

1/4"x 2" IRON STRAPS TWO PER DRUM.

NOTE: MAKE FRAME FIRST, THEN STRAP IN AND SECURE DRUMS. (PAINT WITH "COPPER" IF ON SALT WATER.

PLANK LAST!

ROUND OFF

4 DRUM - 6' x 8'
6 " - 8' x 10'
8 " - 8" x 12'

ANCHOR IN CENTER TO AVOID POSSIBLE FOULING IN CABLE WHEN DIVING

ANCHOR

NOT FASTENED HERE

BLOCK←

IRON YOKE

LAG BOLTS

MAKE DIVING BOARD OF 2"x 12" OAK OR YELLOW PINE.

CDL

20 THINGS FOR

A WEATHER STATION . . .

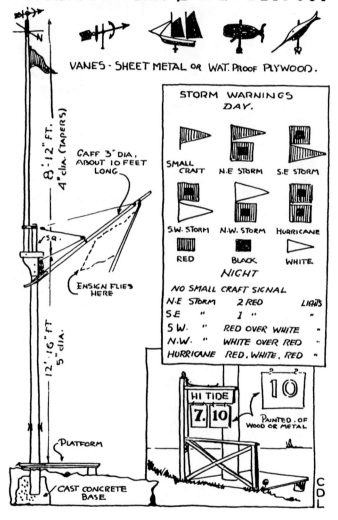

VANES - SHEET METAL OR WAT. PROOF PLYWOOD.

8'-12' FT. 4" dia. (TAPERS)

GAFF 3" DIA. ABOUT 10 FEET LONG

3" SQ.

ENSIGN FLIES HERE

12'-16' FT. 5" dia.

PLATFORM

CAST CONCRETE BASE

STORM WARNINGS DAY.

SMALL CRAFT   N.E STORM   S.E STORM

S.W. STORM   N.W. STORM   HURRICANE

RED   BLACK   WHITE

NIGHT

NO SMALL CRAFT SIGNAL
N.E STORM   2 RED   LIGHTS
S.E "   1 "   "
S.W. "   RED OVER WHITE   "
N.W. "   WHITE OVER RED   "
HURRICANE   RED, WHITE, RED   "

HI TIDE
7.10

10
PAINTED. OF WOOD OR METAL

C D L

A SEA SCOUT OVER-NIGHTER

HOW TO "CRUISE" ON A
SMALL SAIL OR ROWING
BOAT.

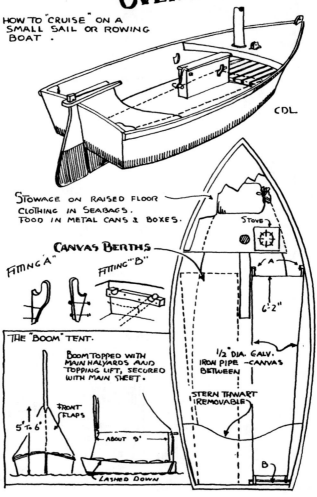

CDL

STOWAGE ON RAISED FLOOR
CLOTHING IN SEABAGS.
FOOD IN METAL CANS & BOXES.

STOVE

CANVAS BERTHS

FITTING "A"   FITTING "B"

A

6'-2"

THE "BOOM" TENT.

BOOM TOPPED WITH
MAIN HALYARDS AND
TOPPING LIFT, SECURED
WITH MAIN SHEET.

1/2" DIA. GALV.
IRON PIPE — CANVAS
BETWEEN

FRONT
FLAPS

STERN THWART
REMOVABLE

5' TO 6'

ABOUT 9'

LASHED DOWN

B

A WOODEN BILGE PUMP.

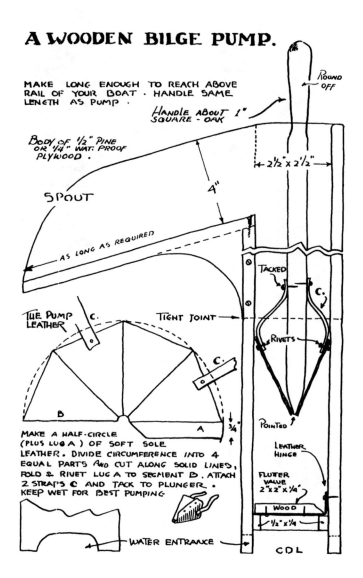

MAKE LONG ENOUGH TO REACH ABOVE RAIL OF YOUR BOAT. HANDLE SAME LENGTH AS PUMP.

Handle about 1" SQUARE - OAK

Round off

BODY of ½" PINE OR ¼" WAT. PROOF PLYWOOD.

SPOUT

← 2½" x 2½" →

4"

AS LONG AS REQUIRED

TACKED

C.

TIGHT JOINT

THE PUMP LEATHER   C.

C.

RIVETS

B

A   ¾"

POINTED

MAKE A HALF-CIRCLE (PLUS LUG A) OF SOFT SOLE LEATHER. DIVIDE CIRCUMFERENCE INTO 4 EQUAL PARTS AND CUT ALONG SOLID LINES, FOLD & RIVET LUG A TO SEGMENT B. ATTACH 2 STRAPS C AND TACK TO PLUNGER. KEEP WET FOR BEST PUMPING.

LEATHER HINGE

FLUTER VALVE 2" x 2" x ¼"

WOOD

½" x ¼"

← WATER ENTRANCE →

CDL

CREWS TO MAKE   213

SHIP CHANDLERY.

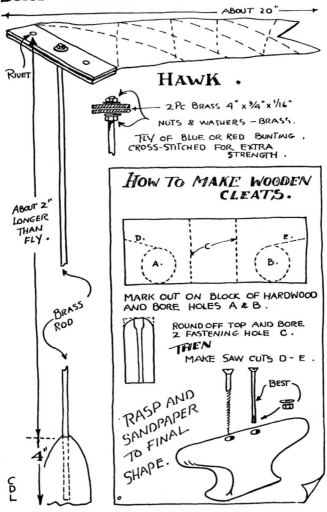

ABOUT 20"

RIVET

HAWK.

2 PC BRASS 4" x ¾" x ¹/16"

NUTS & WASHERS — BRASS.

FLY OF BLUE OR RED BUNTING.
CROSS-STITCHED FOR EXTRA
STRENGTH.

ABOUT 2"
LONGER
THAN
FLY.

BRASS
ROD

4"

C
D
L

HOW TO MAKE WOODEN CLEATS.

D.   C   E.

A.   B.

MARK OUT ON BLOCK OF HARDWOOD
AND BORE HOLES A & B.

ROUND OFF TOP AND BORE
2 FASTENING HOLE C.

THEN

MAKE SAW CUTS D - E.

BEST

RASP AND
SANDPAPER
TO FINAL
SHAPE.

THE CAULKING MALLET

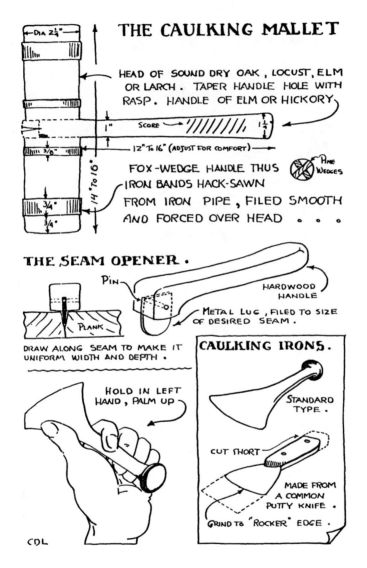

Dia 2¼"

HEAD OF SOUND DRY OAK, LOCUST, ELM OR LARCH. TAPER HANDLE HOLE WITH RASP. HANDLE OF ELM OR HICKORY.

1"   SCORE ➔ ///////// 1¼"

12" To 16" (ADJUST FOR COMFORT)

14" To 16"

FOX-WEDGE HANDLE THUS
IRON BANDS HACK-SAWN
FROM IRON PIPE, FILED SMOOTH
AND FORCED OVER HEAD . . .

FINE WEDGES

3/8"

3/4"
3/4"

THE SEAM OPENER.

PIN

HARDWOOD HANDLE

PLANK

METAL LUG, FILED TO SIZE OF DESIRED SEAM.

DRAW ALONG SEAM TO MAKE IT UNIFORM WIDTH AND DEPTH.

HOLD IN LEFT HAND, PALM UP

CAULKING IRONS.

STANDARD TYPE.

CUT SHORT

MADE FROM A COMMON PUTTY KNIFE.

GRIND TO "ROCKER" EDGE.

CDL

CREWS TO MAKE   **215**

FIDS.

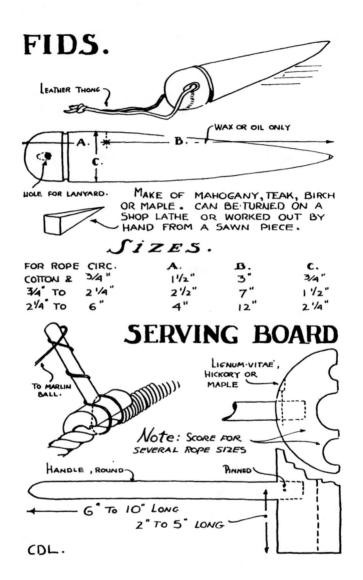

LEATHER THONG

WAX OR OIL ONLY

A. B.

C.

HOLE FOR LANYARD.

MAKE OF MAHOGANY, TEAK, BIRCH OR MAPLE. CAN BE TURNED ON A SHOP LATHE OR WORKED OUT BY HAND FROM A SAWN PIECE.

Sizes.

FOR ROPE CIRC.		A.	B.	C.
COTTON &	3/4 "	1 1/2 "	3 "	3/4 "
3/4 " TO	2 1/4 "	2 1/2 "	7 "	1 1/2 "
2 1/4 " TO	6 "	4 "	12 "	2 1/4 "

SERVING BOARD

TO MARLIN BALL.

LIGNUM·VITAE, HICKORY OR MAPLE

Note: SCORE FOR SEVERAL ROPE SIZES

HANDLE, ROUND

PINNED

6" TO 10" LONG

2" TO 5" LONG

CDL.

20 THINGS FOR

A CRUISING LEAD.

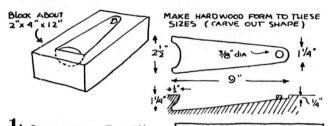

Block ABOUT 2"×4"×12"

MAKE HARDWOOD FORM TO THESE SIZES (CARVE OUT SHAPE)

$2\frac{1}{2}$"   ⅜" dia   1¼"

9"

$\frac{1}{2}$"   1¼"   ¼"

1. POUR ONE HALF WITH HOT LEAD (MELTED PIPE, TINFOIL OR SINKERS). BEFORE HARDENING INSERT 5 BRASS SCREWS AS SHOWN.

2 WHEN COOL, REMOVE FROM MOLD & CAST SECOND HALF. IMMEDIATELY PLACE FIRST HALF OVER IT, IMBEDDING THE SCREWS AND LET THEM BOND TOGETHER.

C D L

"A"

3.

FILE SMOOTH WHEN COOL — ESPECIALLY THE EYE. BORE 2 DOZ. ⅛" HOLES ⅛" DEEP IN BOTTOM CAVITY "A".

SEWN   HEMP

SPLICE AND SERVE WITH LEATHER.

"ARM" BY PRESSING IN TALLOW, WAX, PARAFIN OR PUTTY

THE MARKINGS.

FIRST SOAK LINE IN SEA WATER — THEN STRETCH TAUT.

17 FATH. RED WOOL RAG

2 FATH. LEATHER

7 FATH. RED WOOL RAG

10 FATH. LEATHER, 1 HOLE

3 FATH. LEATHER

15 FATH. WHITE COT. RAG

5 FATH. WHITE COTTON RAG

13 FATH. LEATHER

20 FATH. LINE WITH 2 KNOTS.

A DITTY BOX

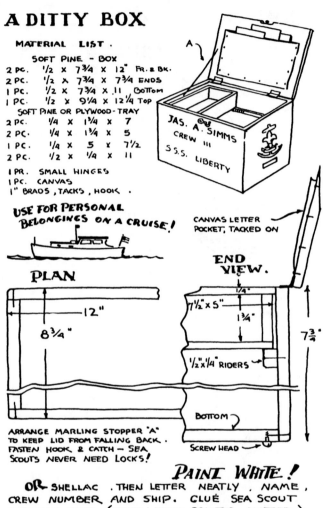

MATERIAL LIST.

SOFT PINE - BOX

2 PC. 1/2 X 7¾ X 12" FR. & BK.
2 PC. 1/2 X 7¾ X 7¾ ENDS
1 PC. 1/2 X 7¾ X 11 BOTTOM
1 PC. 1/2 X 9¼ X 12¼ TOP

SOFT PINE OR PLYWOOD - TRAY

2 PC. 1/4 X 1¾ X 7
2 PC. 1/4 X 1¾ X 5
1 PC. 1/4 X 5 X 7½
2 PC. 1/2 X 1/4 X 11

1 PR. SMALL HINGES
1 PC. CANVAS
1" BRADS, TACKS, HOOK.

JAS. A. SIMMS
CREW 111
S.S.S. LIBERTY

USE FOR PERSONAL BELONGINGS ON A CRUISE!

CANVAS LETTER POCKET, TACKED ON

PLAN

END VIEW.

12"

8¾"

1/4"

7½" X 5"

1¾"

7¾

1/2"X 1/4" RIDERS

ARRANGE MARLING STOPPER "A" TO KEEP LID FROM FALLING BACK. FASTEN HOOK & CATCH — SEA SCOUTS NEVER NEED LOCKS!

BOTTOM

SCREW HEAD

PAINT WHITE!

OR SHELLAC. THEN LETTER NEATLY, NAME, CREW NUMBER AND SHIP. GLUE SEA SCOUT INSIGNIA CUTS (TAKEN FROM PRINTED MATTER) ON BOTH ENDS AND SPAR VARNISH TWO COATS

NAUTICAL BOOK ENDS

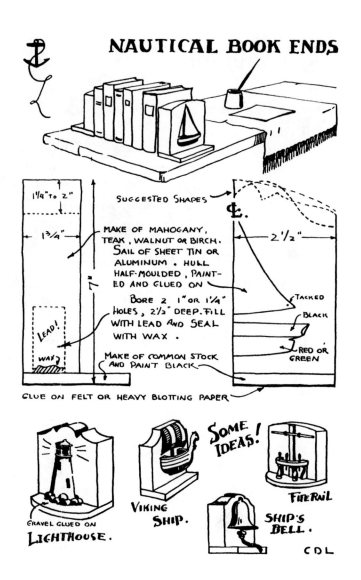

SUGGESTED SHAPES

1¼" TO 2"

1¾"

7"

LEAD!

WAX

MAKE OF MAHOGANY, TEAK, WALNUT OR BIRCH. SAIL OF SHEET TIN OR ALUMINUM. HULL HALF-MOULDED, PAINT-ED AND GLUED ON

BORE 2 1" OR 1¼" HOLES, 2½" DEEP. FILL WITH LEAD AND SEAL WITH WAX.

MAKE OF COMMON STOCK AND PAINT BLACK

℄.

2½"

TACKED

BLACK

RED OR GREEN

GLUE ON FELT OR HEAVY BLOTTING PAPER

GRAVEL GLUED ON
LIGHTHOUSE.

VIKING SHIP.

SOME IDEAS!

FIFERAIL

SHIP'S BELL.

CDL

CREWS TO MAKE   219

SEA SCOUT GIFTS AND SOUVENIRS.

INEXPENSIVE, EASILY MADE ITEMS FOR THE SOCIAL, PARENTS NIGHT OR BRIDGE OF HONOR.

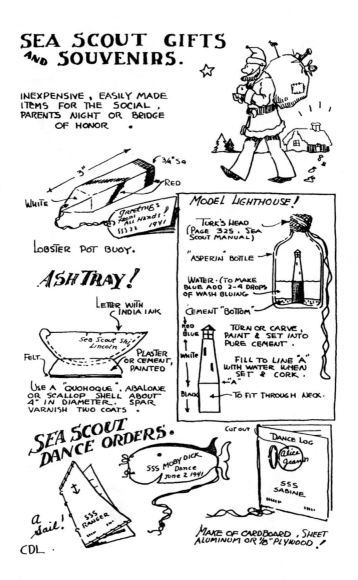

3" ¾" SQ
RED
WHITE

GREETINGS FROM ALL HANDS! SSS 22 1941

LOBSTER POT BUOY.

ASH TRAY!

LETTER WITH INDIA INK

Sea Scout Ship Lincoln

FELT
PLASTER OR CEMENT, PAINTED

USE A "QUOHOQUE", ABALONE OR SCALLOP SHELL ABOUT 4" IN DIAMETER. SPAR VARNISH TWO COATS.

MODEL LIGHTHOUSE!

TURK'S HEAD (PAGE 325, SEA SCOUT MANUAL)

"ASPERIN" BOTTLE

WATER · (TO MAKE BLUE ADD 2-4 DROPS OF WASH BLUING)

CEMENT "BOTTOM"

RED
BLUE
WHITE
BLACK

TURN OR CARVE, PAINT & SET INTO PURE CEMENT.

FILL TO LINE "A" WITH WATER WHEN SET & CORK.

"A"

TO FIT THROUGH NECK.

SEA SCOUT DANCE ORDERS.

SSS MOBY DICK Dance June 2 1941

a Sail!
SSS RANGER

CDL.

CUT OUT
DANCE LOG
Alice Jeanin
SSS SABINE

MAKE OF CARDBOARD, SHEET ALUMINUM OR ⅛" PLYWOOD!

A SALTY DESK SET.

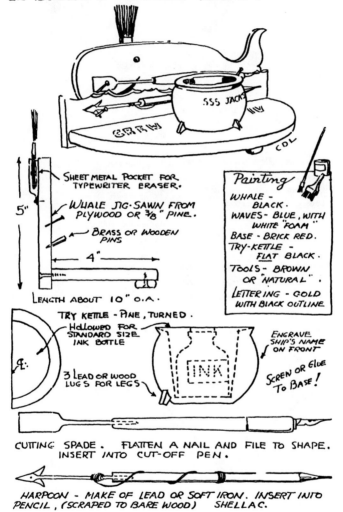

SHEET METAL POCKET FOR
TYPEWRITER ERASER.

WHALE JIG-SAWN FROM
PLYWOOD OR 3/8" PINE.

BRASS OR WOODEN
PINS

5"

4"

LENGTH ABOUT 10" O.A.

Painting

WHALE -
    BLACK.
WAVES- BLUE, WITH
    WHITE "FOAM"
BASE - BRICK RED.
TRY-KETTLE -
    FLAT BLACK.
TOOLS- BROWN
   OR "NATURAL".
LETTERING - GOLD
WITH BLACK OUTLINE

TRY KETTLE - PINE, TURNED.

HOLLOWED FOR
STANDARD SIZE
INK BOTTLE

3 LEAD OR WOOD
LUGS FOR LEGS

INK

ENGRAVE
SHIP'S NAME
ON FRONT

SCREW OR GLUE
TO BASE!

CUTTING SPADE. FLATTEN A NAIL AND FILE TO SHAPE.
INSERT INTO CUT-OFF PEN.

HARPOON - MAKE OF LEAD OR SOFT IRON. INSERT INTO
PENCIL, (SCRAPED TO BARE WOOD) SHELLAC.

CREWS TO MAKE

INDEX

HANDBOOK FOR

HANDBOOK FOR

HANDBOOK FOR

CPSIA information can be obtained at www.ICGtesting.com
Printed in the USA
BVOW04s1652100614

355966BV00006B/63/P